C000141405

The Divine Awakening

The Divine Awakening

by

BROTHER MANDUS

Published by
ARTHUR JAMES LIMITED
THE DRIFT, EVESHAM, WORCS.

©—Brother Mandus —1961
World rights Arthur James Ltd.

No part of this book may be reproduced in any
form whatsoever without written permission
from the publishers, except in cases of brief
quotations used in written reviews and critical
essays printed in newspapers and magazines.

MADE AND PRINTED IN GREAT BRITAIN BY PURNELL AND SONS, LTD.
PAULTON (SOMERSET) AND LONDON

DEDICATION

I humbly dedicate this book to all my friends in the British Isles and Commonwealth, the United States of America and other countries. Only their love, fellowship and prayer have made it possible for me to write about miracles of Divine Healing and this vision for the new Christ Age now dawning.

It is impossible to give acknowledgment of my great indebtedness to each one personally as I would wish, but I pray that the words of this book may truly represent their individual and collective love for the Lord and for each other.

In this united love, our dedication is to the Lord Jesus Christ. Our prayer, and the only purpose of this writing, is that these words may bring healing, inspiration and spiritual quickening to all whom the Lord leads to read them.

Thank You, Father.

The Wind of Change

Introduction by the Rev. John Maillard

"THE WIND OF CHANGE" is a phrase which is being used to describe what is happening in some communities in which a desire for nationhood and sovereignty has been born, and their demand for freedom from serfdom, in order that they may enjoy a standard of life in accordance with their basic human rights.

"The wind of change!" As I read with much interest through this book in manuscript form I found myself thinking of the wind of change which is blowing in another direction, blowing through the Christian Churches, irrespective of denomination, sweeping away some of the traditional teaching we have inherited, traditional teaching which falls short of the Holy Gospel, and sweeping in the Holy and Life-giving Spirit.

In this connection our Holy Lord said, "Howbeit, when he, the Spirit of truth, is come, he will guide you into all truth: for he shall not speak of himself; but whatsoever he shall hear, that shall he speak: and he will shew you things to come. He shall glorify me: for he shall receive of mine, and shall shew it unto you. All things that the Father hath are mine: therefore said I, that he shall take of mine, and shall shew it unto you." A little later the prophecy was fulfilled, "And when the day of pentecost was fully come, they were all with one accord in one place. And suddenly there came a sound from heaven as of a rushing mighty wind, and it filled all the house where they were sitting."

"The wind of change!" A rushing mighty wind sweeping away many of our traditional beliefs regarding sickness, disease, and infirmity, and sweeping in that singleness of mind and purpose which characterizes the Messianic mission of our Lord, and which answers for us the problem of human suffering in relation to the will of God. Our Lord ministered the divine resources of the Kingdom of God to heal the sick and suffering, and in no single instance did He withhold healing, or say or imply that the suffering occasioned by physical diseases was permitted by God for the spiritual growth of those who thus suffered, for chastisement, or for any other spiritual purpose. What He did say was this, "But that the works of God should be made manifest in him, I must work the works of him that sent me, while it is day: the night cometh, when no man can work. As long as I am in the world, I am the light of the world."

However, there is another kind of suffering, the kind which our Lord Himself endured throughout the whole of His public Ministry, and finally at Calvary. Of this suffering He said, "Blessed are they which are persecuted for righteousness' sake: for theirs is the kingdom of heaven."

But there, what is written in this book will speak for itself. and I have no doubt but that its readers will favourably assess its merits in interpreting the ways in which "the wind of change" is affecting the Churches and the world today.

That changes are taking place within the Churches is evident to many observers. One of the ways in which a change is evident is the recovery of the Church's ministry of healing for the body and mind, as well as for the soul, in and through the Person of our Lord and Saviour, Jesus Christ. The Lord Christ is being re-instated in His Church.

It was the saintly Frederick Denison Maurice, a great theologian and a contemporary of Charles Kingsley, who noted that there is a world of difference between knowing and holding fast to the love of God, and knowing that the love of God is holding you. In our own generation it is the difference between a man having his faith in Christ, and a man having Christ in his faith, and, in a larger context, the difference between the Church having its faith in Christ, and the Church having Christ in its faith. This distinction denotes the hallmark of Christianity. It is not sufficient for a man to have faith in Christ: Christ must live in his faith.

The Living and Risen Christ in the faith of man can heal today, as He has healed before. Similarly, the prayer of faith which heals the sick is the faith in which Christ is ever present.

Prayers are dead things, unless Christ is in them. Dead prayers get nowhere: living prayers get everywhere. A prayer for peace is a dead prayer, unless the peace of God is in the prayer. His peace will be in the prayer if His peace is in the hearts of those who offer the prayer. Similarly, a prayer for healing will get through, if the love of god in Christ Jesus is in the prayer.

To revert to the Acts of the Apostles, ch. 2, verse 2—the Birth of the Church. It was the same Holy Spirit which gave birth to our Incarnate Lord which gave birth also to the Church. Without the continuing presence of the Holy Spirit the Church would be nothing more than a moral welfare organisation.

We sing, "The Church's one foundation is Jesus Christ her Lord." And so He is. He is more: He is its life, its inspiration, its healing, its sacraments, its prayers, its worship, its victory, and we, as members of His Mystical Body, are indwelt by His Spirit, to be messengers, ministers, and channels of His Infinite and Perfect Love, for, as the parable of the Vine teaches us, the branch receives its life from the Vine, and we receive our life from the Mystical Body of which we are members incorporate.

I warmly welcome this book by Brother Mandus, and feel it is a privilege to write an introduction to it. I have known the author for many years, and cannot speak too highly of what he has done in giving emphasis to those truths of the Christian Gospel which make it the beacon light of man's salvation. I have attended some of his meetings, and on every occasion his teaching has awakened a consciousness of the

immediacy of the Presence of our Lord to impart new life for
the body and soul.

"Awake thou that sleepest . . . and Christ shall give thee
light."

JOHN MAILLARD

Trusham,
Newton Abbot,
Devon.

Contents

Contents

The Divine Awakening

And he put them all out, and took her by the hand, and called, saying, Maid, arise. And her spirit came again, and she arose straightway: and he commanded to give her meat.

LUKE 8: 54, 55.

THE MOST IMPORTANT NEWS in the world today is that *Divine Healing* is a realistic, scientific and proven fact. Its potential transcends every other modern discovery.

In recent years thousands of people have been healed of every kind of disease through love, faith, prayer and the full acceptance of the Christ Way of life. The impact and significance of these astonishing events is so profound that they open the way into a new age of infinite possibilities for the well-being and creative progression of all mankind.

The central purpose of this book is humbly and simply not only to prove the truth of Divine healing, but to go beyond it by revealing how spiritual principle can prevent disease. And, beyond that again, to describe how prayer, consummated in love and faith, can and must produce the highest creative fulfilment of any life on every level of expression.

The personal stories of Divine healing given in these pages represent but a fragment of the spiritual awakening that is taking place throughout the world. Their place in this book is but to establish for you personally a factual faith, from which you can proceed more realistically to experience the living power of Christ in every aspect of your own life and work.

Since Divine healing is the best of all ways to prove the truth that man can talk to God and receive an answer so potent that it can revolutionise or heal a broken life or body, often spontaneously, I want to begin by reporting one such healing which is beyond medical, scientific, or spiritual doubt.

Countless people in many countries know of the Divine Healing Ministry which has been the life-work of Miss Dorothy Kerin. Her lovely Church of the Healing Christ at Burrswood, Groombridge, Kent, in England, is a focal point of modern healing which has long attracted the interest and support of the Church and many medical practitioners.

The basic significance of her work is that it began through an instantaneous Divine healing which she personally experienced. I have a tape-recording in which she describes this life-saving sacrament, and in her own words this is her story which I have permission to quote.

"Many of you, I expect, have heard how our Lord Jesus Christ laid His hand upon me and restored me instantly to a state of perfect wholeness, after five years of general tuberculosis, which was pathologically and X-ray proved.

"Now I had been an invalid for five years, and during that time everything that medical skill and love and care could do had been done, and I was *in extremis*. Indeed, the doctors who were attending me said that death would occur at any moment. And as my nurse, mother and friends were watching round my bed waiting for the last little flicker of life to ebb away, they saw a great light come around me and they thought it was Jesus taking me. But instead of that they saw me raised to a sitting position, and then they saw my eyes open, and my lips begin to speak. And I said, 'Do you hear? I'm to get up and walk'. Whereupon, I put my hand on the light and got out of bed in the twinkling of an eye, and that after five years a helpless invalid.

"Now there are two significant things about that healing to which I should like to draw your attention for a minute. One is that only because it was the voice of the Living Lord commanding 'Get up and walk' was this dying girl able to do so. Had it been any other voice, nothing would have happened—nothing at all!

"The second point is, that the servant to whom the Lord spoke knew it was the voice of the Lord and without question obeyed, and so the miracle happened. Now that body, which was in such a miserable state, bound up in cotton wool, the next morning was every whit whole—a well, healthy body.

"Doctors came in from all over the world to witness what was called the twentieth-century miracle. They saw the X-ray pictures; they read the pathological report. They consulted the doctors who had been in attendance. And in the end they came to the conclusion that it was *something* beyond their ken. It was a repetition of the raising of Jairus' daughter.

"Now I'm not going to try to make any explanation, medical or spiritual. But I tell you in the presence of God, and before the whole company of Heaven, that those words and those statements are true. You might ask why God singled me out for this miracle. I wish I could answer that question. It certainly was not because of any merit or deserving of my own—no! It was because it was in the Pattern and the Will of God to raise me up for His own purpose. And during the years that have followed we have seen, through the goodness of God, all those miracles in the Bible, all those acts of the apostles; we have seen them all repeated. The wonderful works of God are happening in our midst today. They have never ceased to happen, and they will *never* cease to happen, so long as we have faith and belief in the power of a living, resurrected Christ.

"Why is it, can you tell me, that our hospitals and mental homes are full to overflowing? Much of it is because we lack faith. But if we believed in the living power of a living Lord, we shouldn't be able to get a seat in church. The churches would be crammed to capacity.

"Now that is a challenge to everyone. For God's sake go out into the stricken, suffering, tormented world and tell this message to suffering mankind—that Jesus lives, Jesus walks among us today just as He walked along the shores of Galilee, working miracles, healing the sick, comforting the sorrowing, giving faith to the faithless, giving hope to the hopeless.

"My friends, this is all true. It is not like a book of mystical fiction. It is the truth. It is the truth of God.

"Indeed, I will say, in all humility, that if those miracles which our Lord Jesus wrought nearly 2,000 years ago were true, then they are equally true today. And if they cannot happen today, then the whole thing is a myth and a lie. But, thank God, we know it is true. Jesus Christ is the same—yesterday, today and for ever. Thanks be to God."

*   *   *   *

I deliberately share Miss Dorothy Kerin's story with you because it symbolises the work that is being done, not only in my own ministry, but in every denomination, wherever faith and love become quickened to embrace the concept of the Lord's response and intervention in human affairs.

Even this one Divine healing is sufficient, potentially, to change the pattern of life throughout the world. It is a challenge and invitation to every church, doctor, scientist, politician and everyman to recognise and undertake research into the principles which make such an experience possible.

In an intellectually awakening generation, it is a sacrilege just to shrug our shoulders and ignore the significance of such transcendental evidence. It is nothing less than an affront to human intelligence and integrity to bypass the need to discover how such healings can take place.

The Church already holds the truth in the life and teaching of Jesus Christ. The medical profession is committed to healing and, as never before, undertakes research to this end. Doctors cannot much longer fail to recognise the need to break free from preconceived ideas and to embark on a research programme which accepts the fact that man is indeed a trinity of spirit, mind and body, part of the One Spirit of the universe.

Now that we can prove healing follows faith and prayer, it is essential to introduce a concentrated research into the laws which govern the response of the Creator to meet the urgent needs of man.

My travels have taken me far and wide in the world, conducting Divine healing services, and I have constantly observed the action of God healing and helping those who were sick or in trouble. I will report some of these experiences in this book.

But, more important, is the witness to the Divine Awakening which is quickening the spiritual scene everywhere. There has not been so much interest in Christianity and spiritual development for hundreds of years as there is today.

Despite the outward dangers and turbulence, and the constant threat of war, millions of people are beginning to understand that the only real answer to the personal, national and international problems of this age inevitably lies within the orbit of spiritual principle. In fact, the common people are, generally speaking, now ready and yearning to be led boldly into a full recognition and practice of the full gospel of Jesus Christ.

In the United States there has never been such an intensive awakening as that which is now in progress. Throughout the British Isles and the Commonwealth millions of people know about Divine healing and long for a united acceptance and teaching of the true ways of prayer.

On the continent of Europe, in the West Indies and South Africa I have witnessed much of this hunger for spiritual truth.

Wherever I travel, ministers and people are feeling this tremendous sense of revival in the spiritually new scientific approach. They are united in this sensing of the new Christ Age, and the awakening of man to the truth that without God he is nothing.

During a recent mission to New Zealand I caught the vision of an entire country potentially arising to become a Holy Land of holy people. And, in the mysterious ways of God, how wonderful it will be when the first nation awakens comprehensively to demonstrate a total allegiance to the Father! It could lead the whole world back to safety and sanity, and prove the abundant life which Jesus proclaimed to be the destiny of man.

The Signs and Wonders which are increasing day by day represent the dawn of a new age. And the most significant fact is that this is nothing less than a *Divine* Awakening in which the whole world is involved. We have reached the next phase in human evolution and it is the Father Who inspires the new vision that is being quickened into action throughout the entire Church in every denomination, and among people everywhere.

Man's search for freedom is his constant driving power. Instinctively he not only seeks this freedom through materialistic ways, but inwardly yearns for the freedom of the spirit in the eternal reality of his life in the spirit of God.

In the new awakening, and more realistically than ever before, religion, science and the arts find a common cause and recognition of their absolute partnership in the exploration and experience of Divine truth in every field of human endeavour.

I lovingly dedicate this book to the children of the new Christ Age, and embrace them all through the three little ones who were healed in South Africa by prayer, and whose story I tell in the next chapter.

I pray that, as you read, you too will be increasingly aware of the simple fact that you are doing so in the Presence of God, in Whose spirit you live, and move, and have your being.

I pray, in the Name of Jesus Christ, that you may be inspired to take your rightful place as a son or daughter of God in the Divine Awakening of the abundant life and brotherhood of all mankind.

2

The Sleeping Children

*As for me, I will behold thy face in righteousness: I shall
be satisfied, when I awake, with thy likeness.*

PSALM 17: 15.

THE FIRST PLAINTIVE CRY of a new-born baby
awakening to life on earth is alive with the power of
creation to all who hear it. Mothers and fathers,
doctors, midwives and nurses quicken with an emotion of love
unsullied by the things of this world and are very close to
God as they behold His handiwork.

Only a mother, perhaps, can experience the full rapture
of sharing with God the bearing and birth of a new life. The
thrill of conception is but the prelude to a heavenly consummation, as her own child quickens in the womb to awaken
her tenderness and care. And every mother, when she cradles
the baby to her breast, is really experiencing the ecstasy of
God's fulfilment through her.

This miracle is the central revelation of the Father's power
and presence amongst His world family. In this, we are
personally involved in an eternal creative process which we
observe and experience. Borne on an irresistible tide of
creative power, millions of new lives come into being every
year. Every second of the day and night babies are arriving
in every land on earth, every one of them demonstrating
the Almighty Spirit in Whom we live, move, and have our
being.

There are about three thousand million people on earth
now. It is a sobering thought to realise that we all came into
being through the womb of life, absolutely dependent upon

the Father for everything, always. We all uttered our first cry. We all needed our mother's love and protection. And we shall all be awakened in God's Spirit again when we pass through the portals of death into the next plane.

In the inward and vital reaches of life we are all one in God. The outward pressures and turmoils are quite false to our true nature. Whether we are born in a kraal in central Africa, in an igloo in the Arctic, an apartment in San Francisco, a workman's cottage or a castle in England, we must all be equal in God's Spirit, for we are the self-evident product of His own being and purpose.

It has been said that we are closer to God in a garden than anywhere else. It is true, of course, that we can surely behold the majesty of Divine action in every aspect of creation, and every blade of grass, flower or tree is telling us the same story. But I venture to suggest that we can probably become more intensely aware of God's Presence when we hold a child in our arms, in prayer, than in any other way. Let me tell you why.

Everyone will agree that babies and young children never fail to stir us with their beauty and purity. They reveal their own Divine nature in a thousand ways, completely untarnished, as yet, by the ways of the world. They are, in fact, still clearly manifesting God's Love. They offer us an open door through which we, too, can pass into His Presence.

As a small boy, about seven years old, I used to have some extraordinary experiences which only now do I fully understand. Quite often, even in the midst of exciting activities like playing with my toys, I would be "caught up" in an intense stillness, and during such moments was always aware of a wondrous Presence. Sometimes I felt as though I was being lifted right away into heights far removed from my room of play.

These experiences were always accompanied by a tremendous joy which even then gave me a most comforting sense that I was very much loved. I never saw any visions, apart from waves of intense violet light which gave the impression of infinite extension. Once, after one of these periods in the Great Stillness, I went straight to a huge mirror in a very broad gilt frame hanging over the mantelpiece, and, boy-like, scratched with a nail on the gold paint words which have been etched on my soul as eternal truth ever since: "I will never die. God loves me."

These periods of stillness gradually diminished, and it was not until many years later that I re-discovered what I now realise to be deep meditation in the Presence of God. But I do know now that young children are very close to the Lord and that wise parents and friends can help them, and themselves, in Christ-like ways by communion with the Lord together in perfect love, faith, trust and expectancy.

After learning much about human problems in the course of many years devoted to business, I became completely committed to our Lord and Saviour Jesus Christ, and yearned only to follow Him in the full Gospel of love, faith, prayer and healing. And soon I was guided, in the midst of great personal tribulations, and without any money, to open a Sanctuary of Divine Healing based on absolute love for God, and people, and devoted entirely to helping anyone, without condition or price, even as Jesus would do.

I soon discovered that the "signs and wonders" followed this simple love, faith and prayer, as Jesus promises in all His teaching. As bruised and broken people began to come to my first humble two-roomed sanctuary, and we prayed together, they were transformed. Sometimes an instantaneous healing would occur and we would marvel at such a revelation of the living Presence. Sometimes our prayers produced only a betterment of the condition, and many healings were only effected finally after weeks of prayer and devotion to the Christ Way of life. Some people were never healed physically, but in most cases the miracle of spiritual transformation took place.

The first person who came to the Sanctuary for help was an elderly lady with crippling arthritis in her legs. We simply prayed together in love and a simple faith that Christ's Perfection was in our midst. Ten minutes later she just got on to her feet and walked absolutely free.

I knew then at the outset that not only were my own dedication and faith justified, but that here was, potentially, the complete answer to every human ill—from warfare right down to personal problems and pains. And, after all, this is exactly what Jesus revealed in His good news for mankind.

Naturally enough, with the Lord in charge, the work rapidly expanded through the years and, by the Grace and direction of God alone, it has become a world ministry of love, prayer, and spiritual teaching. My guidance, from the beginning, was to establish a World Healing Crusade dedicated absolutely to help all people, and all churches, in a strictly inter-denominational way without any conditions attaching to our service.

There is a wondrous freedom in Christ's Love when we depend upon Him for everything, from supply to complete direction in every phase of our lives. In this love we are not interested in magnifying our own organisation but rather in advancing the work of the Lord in every other church or group. The result of this has been that we have no churches or personal interests. We have become simply a channel through which love, prayer, free literature, free recordings and free services pour out from the Father to people and churches in many areas of the world.

I mention all this only because it is a witness to the dynamics of Christ's Power, in that He was able to use so inadequate a person as myself in such service. He worked just the same miracle with so many of His first disciples and people of the early Church, and continues to do so today in the Divine Awakening which is quickening the entire Christian community.

In my case, without any canvassing or personal effort, I was invited to conduct Divine healing services in many churches. And, down the years, this has resulted in thousands of services in churches of most denominations throughout the British

Isles, on the Continent, in the United States, Canada, West
Indies, South Africa and New Zealand. Each year the work
has grown.

All this travelling and service in prayer naturally provides
a wide experience of God's Love in action. It is simply true
that He has healed thousands of diseased and broken lives—
not by any power of our own, but by His Spirit responding
to the love and faith offered to Him when we are in prayer.

This brings me to the story I want to tell about the "Sleeping Children", and explains why I was travelling on a Divine
healing mission throughout South Africa where these particular healings occurred.

Very often, in Divine healing services, I have to take young
children in my arms in prayer. For me this is the highest
pinnacle of love and Christ-awareness I ever reach. When I
stand before a congregation of perhaps a thousand people
with a child in my arms we know that His Spirit is with us
in the intense Stillness which enfolds us all. And, as the
people pray, the feeling of Perfection shining through the
little life I am holding is an experience of God's Love which
no words can ever describe. At such moments one realises
that it is incredible that anyone, anywhere, could even try
to live without a perfect faith in God.

So I was leading Divine healing services in South Africa.
In one service a little boy, about six years old, was given into
my arms, fast asleep. The parents told me he was suffering
from five or six epileptic fits every day. All the people prayed.
And the child, still sleeping, was returned to his parents.

Later in Stutterheim, the Methodist minister, the Rev. W. F.
Brennan, and his wife brought their little girl Gail for healing
prayer. She, too, was fast asleep. She was suffering from de-
formed feet. We all prayed, God was present, and Gail was
handed back to her father.

Then in Cape Town a young mother and father, Mr. and
Mrs. McClure, travelled five hundred miles to bring their
young daughter to another Divine healing service. She had a
crippled leg through polio. This child, too, was fast asleep and

I knew, while holding her in my arms, that something wonderful was happening. Still sleeping, she was given back to her parents.

At that time I did not know in any outward or visible way the result of our prayers. But a year later, on my return to South Africa for another mission, each of these families came to tell me how their child had been healed at the earlier healing services.

The little boy who had been suffering five or six epileptic fits each day never had another throughout the year following that moment of prayer. Fast asleep, enfolded in the love, faith and prayer of many people, touched by Christ, he had simply awakened to a new life of wholeness.

The significance for mankind, of even that one healing, is of such scientific importance that research and practice by Church and doctors could open wide the New Age that is dawning. And thousands of case histories of Divine healing have been reported in recent years by ministers and people of every denomination!

Then I met again the Methodist minister, the Rev. W. F. Brennan, and his wife, for whose daughter Gail we had prayed the previous year. In this case a tape recording was taken of the talk I had with them, and also with the orthopaedic surgeon who had previously attended Gail, thus emphasising the importance of their witness. This, and all other recordings quoted in this book, are in my possession and available for reference. This is what Mr. Brennan said:

"May I go back to the time when Gail first began to walk. Immediately she took the first stumbling step my wife noticed something wrong. We finally decided we'd better go and have a check-up with a specialist. Fortunately, we were on holiday and we went to see the doctor. He was very pleased that we took the baby, and said that if she wasn't seen to now something would happen and she would never be able to walk properly. He told us that it would be a very long-drawn-out treatment, and prescribed special

boots for her—surgical boots. We had to go to the orthopaedic workshop and have them made. As we lived over
ninety miles from East London and had to get new boots
every two months or ten weeks, it was very expensive. It
meant that we had to go down and see the doctor, have the
child measured for the boots, then return home again, and
then go back in about a week's time for the boots. It very
often meant going down about three times in all, and the
boots would only last about two months or ten weeks.

"And then, when you came out to the country, you were
lecturing at the Ministers' Retreat in Stutterheim. That
evening we had the Divine healing service in the Town
Hall.

"When you made the appeal for anyone to come forward
for healing, little Gail was sleeping in my arms, and I
handed the baby over to you. She continued sleeping, and
you blessed her and handed her back to me. From that
moment we noticed there was a great improvement in her.
In fact, we never went back to the specialist again. She
never wore surgical boots from that day. Soon she was able
to run about and be quite normal, like any other child."

Mr. Brennan then went on to describe a healing which he
also experienced at the same time:

"I suffered for about twenty years with sinus trouble. I
had the operation, and at various times had the sinus
flushed out. But it always recurred. Of late years I lived
with Aspros and the special drops—anything to give me
relief. About six or seven times during the winter months
I was laid up with sinus and severe headaches.

"That evening of the healing service in Stutterheim, after
we felt that Gail had been healed, I also stood up and
claimed a healing for my sinus. It didn't go away immediately, but over a period of two or three weeks I could feel
it getting better every day, until finally I had no more headaches. It was wonderful. I should also testify to a 'glow' that

my wife and I experienced, because for about three or four days afterwards I could feel that 'warmness' within me. I knew that I was healed from my sinus trouble."

When the Brennans offered their child Gail to the Lord it was as though this opened the way for healing to touch all their lives, because simultaneously with her husband Mrs. Brennan was also renewed. This is how she described her experience:

"As I told you, I definitely felt a warm 'glow' within me, and knew that Gail's feet were completely healed.

"Well, last year when you were up here I was expecting my second child. I had to go to my doctor for a check-up. He was away, and I had to be attended to by his colleague. After he had examined me, he told me that my heart was 'kaput'. He put it in just those words. It was finished. I had to rest. I had to take it absolutely easy.

"Well, it shocked me. I was really very, very scared. And then I went to see the doctor in Sterkstroom where we lived, and he told me the same thing. We attended your healing service in Queenstown two or three days after that. And that night I claimed healing. But it was something you said that convinced me that my heart was healed. You said that God gives life even to a grain of sand, and I knew then that God could give life to my heart. And He did. Because when I went back the following month to have the monthly check-up with my doctor who was back from his holiday, he looked at my card after examining me and said, 'I don't know why my colleague put this on your card, because there is nothing wrong with your heart. Your heart is sound.' I had the other doctor check my heart again, and he said, 'Here I've made a note in my book that your heart was definitely very irregular, and it was very tired. Now I find nothing wrong with it at all'."

There is an important confirmation in connection with the healing of Gail's feet.

A few days prior to recording the Brennan story I had arrived in East London. A group of ministers, their wives and friends were assembled to welcome me by invitation of Mr. and Mrs. Gordon-Davis of the Grace Dieu Healing Sanctuary. Among the guests were the Brennan family and an orthopaedic surgeon. For medical ethical reasons I cannot divulge his name, so shall call him Mr. X. While moving round the circle in greeting, I looked across the room and saw Mr. X closely examining Gail's legs and feet. I was told that he was the orthopaedic surgeon who had been treating her prior to the Divine healing. Later I talked with him about it and recorded his views. This is what Mr. X said:

"This little child was brought to me when she first started to walk. I remember her very well. She had a congenital flat foot. Actually, both feet were involved, and it was necessary for me to prescribe surgical boots and arch supports. Normally, this type of condition takes several years before an improvement is noted. I've seen her at fairly regular intervals, but until recently I hadn't seen the child for well over twelve months. I met Mr. and Mrs. Brennan last week and heard the story of how, after having attended one of Brother Mandus' Divine healing services, they had noted that little Gail's feet seemed quite normal. I asked if I might examine the feet, and it is perfectly true that I could find no abnormality. Her feet were quite normal.

"Of course I cannot say what transpired between the time that I last saw Gail until I recently examined her. But I know, because of other experiences, that something which we cannot understand or explain from a purely scientific point of view does take place. There are things, from a medical or scientific point of view, for which we have no explanation. Apart from that, as Christians, if we believe what Jesus said two thousand years ago, all things are possible by prayer, and I see no reason why the miracles of Christ's day should not occur today.

"I think there should be more co-operation between ministers and doctors. Man is not composed only of flesh and blood. He is a trinity of mind, soul and body. I think that the minister and the doctor should co-operate wherever possible in matters pertaining to the spirit, mind and body."

I asked Mr. X if he had ever had any personal experience of the power of prayer helping him in his operations and medical work, to which he replied:

"Yes, I try to take God into my work for I realise, to quote the words of Jesus, that 'I of mine own self can do nothing'. I feel inspired sometimes and guided in the making of a diagnosis, or in the correct management and treatment of a case. I make mistakes, of course. But when I feel within me something which is intangible but, I don't know, I suppose you would call it an elevation of mood, then I do my best work.

"The medical profession is a noble one, and its aims and principles, which amount to alleviating the sickness of humanity, must be founded basically on the principle of love. And that, as I have come to learn, is the most important spiritual principle. I have found a number of my colleagues who more and more are coming to realise the importance of high principles and bringing them into practice in their medical work."

Later I moved to Cape Town to conduct there services in the Metropolitan Methodist, Congregational and Presbyterian churches. Mr. and Mrs. McClure, who brought their daughter Robin to the service the previous year, again came five hundred miles to meet me. But this time they came, not for healing, but to give thanks for the complete healing of their child following their previous journey of faith.

I was deeply moved, and very humble, before this sincerity and dedication, and we did indeed give thanks to the Father for changing their child's life. People are wonderful, always,

but when they are truly touched by Christ we can see clearly
God's plan and purpose for His world family.

The McClure story really began in a place with the strange
name of "Wilderness", in South Africa, where exotic flowers
and trees clothe the coastal hills. The little town of Wilderness nestles unspoilt on the slopes rising from a sun-warmed
beach—consisting only of a scattering of villas and beautiful
gardens. A little church on the hill nearby, surrounded by
green lawns, reminded me of one in a Cotswold village in
England.

Trees everywhere, a perfect climate, and looking down from
many of these houses you can see the big breakers coming in
from the Indian Ocean—tumbling and creamy white in the
sunshine. A large lake fills a valley and almost meets the
ocean across a bar of golden sand.

Mrs. McClure and her little girl Robin were visiting her
sister-in-law, Mrs. Grant, who had received some books describing the work of the World Healing Crusade. These had
awakened her interest in Divine healing. Mrs. McClure told
me what then transpired in these words:

"Well, when my sister-in-law read out these papers to
me I was very interested, but it just didn't occur to me
immediately that it could be for my own child. Then, I
thought, 'If it's for other people, why not for my girl?'
She had had polio. She was wearing a full-length caliper, and
I'd be so glad to see her lose it. She was such a little baby.
I think she was about a year old when we brought her to you.

"Well, we were too late to go to the meeting in Port
Elizabeth where we lived, so my husband drove us down
to Cape Town but he had to return the very next day. He
couldn't come to the meeting. So I took my little baby
along. During the service you held her in your arms,
blessed her, and prayed for her speedy healing. Today,
when she plays among other children, you would never be
able to pick her out. She is so healed that there is no
difference.

"When we returned home after the service we started taking her caliper off for an hour every day, the next week two hours. And so it went on. It was about six weeks or two months when we decided that her caliper was quite unnecessary."

I then asked Mr. McClure to give me his version and recorded his reply:

"Well, my feelings were similar to those of my wife. When we were at Wilderness we believed that healing had happened to other people, but we didn't think immediately in terms of our own child. At this particular stage we were rather despondent because specialists in Port Elizabeth had got to the stage of telling us there was little hope of a natural recovery, and that they were considering surgery. When it was proposed that we go to Cape Town to attend the service at Rondebosch, we made the arrangements. Then I was left on tenterhooks for about five days before my wife returned to give me the news. We didn't see an immediate sign of any improvement, but over the days that improvement did appear. It was a very steady improvement, and when next we went to the specialist for a check-over he was quite amazed at the progress she had made.

"In Port Elizabeth they have a special home where all cripples and children stricken with polio are taken for treatment. Well, there were several children like our own, of the same age, and affected as our Robin. And the progress in them, if any, was barely visible for very many months. After we returned from Cape Town and the service in Rondebosch, Robin's rapid progress was quite obvious as compared with those children who had not had the opportunity of attending a service of healing."

These, then, are the stories of the three "Sleeping Children". Their awakening in the Perfection of God is like the Golden Gates of Heaven swinging wide open, inviting us all to enter this Paradise that has been prepared for us from the beginning.

As long as the Father continues to bless our lives with babies, we can be absolutely sure of the safe and wondrous unfolding of man's eternal destiny as the sons and daughters of God.

I travelled back to England deeply aware of the problems of Africa, but inspired by the spiritual yearning and response of so many churches and people in their search for true solutions.

*   *   *   *

Thank You, Father. In thy healing of these children we recognise the truth revealed by our Lord Jesus Christ, and pray for all children and their parents everywhere. Help us, Lord, in our personal relationships with these little ones to bear them always before Thee with love and faith in Thy Perfection.

We become still now, Father, in Thy Holy Presence. . . . And thankfully realise Thy Healing Love shining in those for whom we pray. In Christ we behold Thy Spirit within them and accept completely that infinite Good is flowing through each life now and constantly in the right way, according to Thy Will and knowledge concerning their eternal well-being. . . .

In all simplicity of trust we release them into Thy care and know it is being done.

And we pray for Africa that all her people may be awakened to fulfil Thy Will for Peace, Harmony and Love, through Jesus Christ our Lord. Amen.

3

Behold, I Make All Things New

Therefore if any man be in Christ, he is a new creature: old things are passed away: behold, all things are become new.

2 CORINTHIANS 5: 17.

I AM WRITING THESE WORDS sitting in my car on the promenade at Blackpool, on the north-west coast of England. It is midwinter. Wrapped up in rugs and hot-water bottles, nourished by flask-hot soup and sandwiches, I am cosily looking out to the wide horizon of ocean and sky. The sun is shining between the white cumulus clouds, and a fresh wind splashes the waves of a high tide across the promenade parapet.

The restless combers break sparkling in the sunshine and make a vivid picture, set in the blue of the sky, which any artist would love to paint. A few people, well protected in warm overcoats, pass by from time to time and they, with me, must be savouring the peace and power of the ozone-laden air. Beyond the horizon lies the Isle of Man, and beyond that again Ireland. Then three thousand miles of turbulent ocean to the eastern coasts of the United States and Canada. And the great ships of sea and air bear an endless tide of people, in a coming and going which embraces practically every aspect of human enterprise and relationship.

How small our world has become to the traveller! By jet plane London to New York—six hours. New York to San Francisco or Los Angeles—six hours. To the other side of the world, east or west, in another handful of hours. And soon, no doubt, we shall have rocket planes and space ships. All this, and a million things more, constantly magnify our experience through the invisible power of human minds, intent on creating greater and ever greater expression of man's infinite and invincible nature.

An important lesson can always be learned by anyone, no matter how evolved or humble the intellect, who cares (or dares) to pause long enough to consider the miracle of mind, its central significance in human achievement, and its inevitable relationship with the infinite Mind of God which makes every aspect of creation and the experience of man possible at all.

The most urgent need of all people today is to turn their attention inwards to seek a deeper understanding of this mental mystery, and its tremendous powers in the creativeness that is certainly man's heritage.

Hypnotized, as we are, by the outward flow of events and things we create, we tend to forget the mighty powers of love, imagination, will and intellect which are the motivating causes of every effect we have ever seen or experienced. Behind the Taj Mahal, the citadels of New York, St. Paul's Cathedral in London, the ships and planes, machines and every building, are the invisible minds which patterned them long before they could be expressed in material form.

The very chair upon which we sit, or the artist's picture we behold, could never exist apart from the thinker who first found the pattern in his mind. The thought, therefore, was the vital factor and, inevitably, the product of chair or picture will always conform to and express the invisible motivating love, imagination and thought.

It becomes increasingly clear that the supreme objective of man must be towards the highest development of his inward faculties, because his life achievements will be governed strictly by the potency of his mind and the degree of his ability to react powerfully to the environment and people through which his potential must unfold.

There is, of course, nowadays an urgent and rapid development of education in every land upon earth. It has long been known that illiteracy is a great obstacle to progress in a modern society. Concentrated efforts are being made in countries like India, China, Africa, Russia and the Middle East generally to develop the intellect of their peoples. In all the more advanced nations, all creative progress has exactly followed the patterns which education opened to them.

Man, the thinker, is awakening *en masse* now with a speed that staggers the imagination, and often affrights us all. In the last hundred years he has advanced his intellectual capacities and corresponding knowledge more than in all the preceding thousands of years of his long climb from the cave to the modern city.

Unfortunately, so much of his mental development has been achieved without regard to the basic spiritual principles and laws which inevitably govern his entire existence. Just as the jet plane in the skies represents the jet-plane thinker, so is the thinker himself the outward form of the Invisible Thinker of the entire universe.

It begins to look like good practical commonsense that we must identify ourselves, and our personal and world creativeness, with the Mind, Spirit, Christ, God, through Whose Being we all exist and through Whom we have any capacity to think at all.

We live, however, in a very exciting and adventurous age. We are actually beginning now the next phase of development. In the very early periods of awakening our long-past forbears concentrated mainly on survival. Slowly they evolved better ways of obtaining food and shelter, and art began to appear. Isolated tribes found greater power and protection by merging together and communities began to grow. The story of the birth of nations is an age-long history of awakening man but, even today, we have not outgrown our animal natures, still so dangerously reflected through our wars, armaments and economic strife.

Always, in the midst of an ever-increasing sense of power

and material objectives, inspired leaders have provided their people with the vision of spiritual truth and principle. All the great religions on earth have stressed these basic factors in human nature.

Then came Jesus Christ with the highest, most profound and yet the simplest spiritual revelation the world has ever known. Here, indeed, was the revelation of love, faith, atonement, redemption and eternal life in which is the salvation of man, and it reaches its highest expression in the Cross of Christ as the way of life divinely ordained for man.

Alas, the greater our education and the corresponding sense of power and personal security, the less are we inclined to think of our need to develop the spiritual aspects of our nature. Until recent times, religion has been in a decline and the vision of the perfect society, living in Christ, was more or less buried beneath an avalanche of self-power and possessions which have become the supreme objectives of the individual and of nations. In fact, national enterprise in every field of activity is concentrated to this end. The Church, still standing, thank God and those who held fast through it all, lost much of her authority and surrendered her leadership in the cause of Christ for which she stood.

But today a new Light is appearing on the horizon. All over the world a spiritual awakening is taking place. A new army of disciples has arisen, both within and outside the Christian Church. They come with new vision and report "Signs and Wonders" very similar to the works of Christ and the early Church.

In this age of intellectual enlightenment, the approach of these new disciples to the exploration of spiritual principles and prayer has been highly scientific. They sought their knowledge in human lives and observed the causes of so much tribulation, disaster and disease.

Beginning from the concept of communion with God, they analysed and traced through countless experiments the fact that an astonishing percentage of physical disease was caused by lack of love, frustration, fear, worry, resentment, sin, and any kind of negative attitude to people, environment or events; and that an equally astonishing degree of healing took place when people were helped to practise the Presence of God in love, faith and prayer.

A library of books has been written proclaiming their findings in this supremely important field of research. Thousands of case histories witness to the truth of Divine healing, and to the simple fact that man cannot live satisfactorily by bread alone. He is a spiritual being, living in a spiritual universe, dependent FIRST upon God for everything. Our common discovery has been that Love, in all its manifold forms of expression, and a child-like faith in God, are the absolute essentials of life itself.

The impact of so many cases of Divine healing is so potent that we can never retrace our steps into the darkness. This new recognition of the power of love, positive prayer and spiritual principle is beginning to sweep through the world. It heralds the dawn of the new Christ Age for which man has ever yearned.

We are indeed in a unique position today. Not only do we have the authority of spiritual leaders based, as it is, on concrete results which touch people at their most sensitive point in world-pervading sickness, but in all the sciences we are meeting the same need to look beyond matter to Mind.

The doctor begins to search for spiritual-mental-emotional causes, while he seeks to heal the distorted or diseased physical cells. The psychiatrist knows already the pressures which disrupt the conscious mind and body, and that these are often so intense that they can produce terrible mental disasters and physical disease. He, too, is involved in a leap from the personal conscious and sub-conscious mind of the patient to a communion with Divine Mind, in order to release the complete healing and integrating factors inherent in spiritual principle and prayer.

With the advent of nuclear physics, the old belief in a materialistic universe has been exploded for ever. As the scientist, in every branch of research, probes deeper into matter, he meets the invisible but all-powerful laws which govern its appearance. He is committed, however reluctantly, to an exploration in the realm of invisible CAUSE, into the very Mind of God. And this, without question, some day will lead him to conceive and believe that LOVE is the central motivating power in all creation, and that communion with Infinite Intelligence can only become known through the ever-widening reach of personal love, faith and prayer.

As Fawcett says: "The universe begins to look more like a great thought than a great machine."

The economic system of our modern society will also come into a new era of expansion and creativeness when Divine laws are fully understood. It has long been a fallacy that "big business" and spiritual principles are in opposing camps. In our new understanding, it becomes clear that any business can only be infinitely more successful for everyone concerned when it is directed and expressed through love, faith and prayer which release infinite GOOD into everything without exception.

We move into a new age of such heights of potential and understanding that the next great concentration of personal, national and international aspiration will be to develop as quickly as possible the scientific use of spiritual principle in every aspect of education. We know already that the Christ-filled mind is infinitely more potent in its creative power than a mind, however highly developed intellectually, that is divorced from an awareness and expression of spiritual principles.

The essence of our modern discoveries is the intensely practical nature of all that Jesus Christ revealed. Here is the complete answer to poverty and disease, when we learn fully how to conform to the Laws which govern a divine response to our needs. Here is the secret of inspiration, guidance and higher creativeness on every level. Here we have the true way to peace on earth, the feeding of the starving millions, the health and well-being of every soul on earth. As a demonstrated reality, as a potential awaiting our exploration and acceptance, is the abundant life which, after all, is what everyone is so feverishly seeking.

All this, and much more, lies awaiting our quickening vision when we pause long enough to interpret the significance and implication of Divine healing.

Wonderful though healing by love, faith and prayer is, it can never be the final objective of spiritual teaching and aspiration. Certainly, if we are sick, it is good to know that in God we can find the healing of both cause and effect. But the wider vision will always be directed to the kind of life we can live when we enter the Christ dimension of consciousness, thus preventing the onslaught of disease, and become able increasingly to fulfil our infinite potentials.

If communion with God is possible, and we categorically state that modern research in prayer has proved it to be so, then we must logically begin to consider what is the true pattern and high objective in our personal life, when thus open to all the love and infinite resources of God.

If we follow the teaching of Jesus Christ, we are told that "all things are possible". From beginning to end of His Word we are taught that according to our faith and love the Father will bring infinite and perfect everything into our experience. We do not need to depart from one word of His life and Gospel to enter into the dynamic experience of God's Power flooding our lives with Good.

It would seem that our only real need is to believe completely in what is taught, and to lift the vision of our faith to accept and expect "mighty works". As long as we continue to limit ourselves by the range of our personal power and vision, we can *only* experience life on that level. Jesus tells us that the Power great enough to mould universes and all life, is not only able, but willing, to come into the little human life and transform it through His strength.

When we seriously begin to "dream our dreams" with God, and link our imagination with His Almighty thinking, then we shall see the outward signs of His Power working through us, just as presently we see the outward results of our own thinking.

In the Father lies all the knowledge of all the laws of creation. There is only one Power, and His Spirit fills everything that ever was or will be, including you and me. With Jesus, we can truly believe "the Kingdom of Heaven is within you" and "All that I have is thine".

In Him we live, and move, and have our being. "Behold, I make all things new." "It is the Father Who doeth the works."

*   *   *   *

The tide has gone back over the sands while I have been writing. The pools are glistening in the afternoon sunlight and the wind has dropped to a gentle breeze. There is, in fact, on this first day of February, quite a feeling of resurrection. It will soon be springtime again in England, and the Father will thrust forth His Life in a surge of splendour, as He clothes the countryside with buds and flowers and all nature will continue to reveal His love and power.

It is this kind of change that is coming upon the people of the world. It is the Father Who is revealing the next phase of His children's development. As we move towards the pinnacle of intellectual awareness and power, so does He now promote the vision and incentive to move into the culminating phase of progression.

There is a feeling of expectancy everywhere among spiritually awakened people. As I travel about the world I meet them in their thousands. Almost every minister I have met in recent years feels a "spirit of revival". People talk openly of the "Second coming of Christ". And, in a thousand ways, the theme of positive Christianity is bringing back a flame very like the enthusiasm and dedication which electrified the early Church.

It is interesting that this sense of revival is not confined to any particular denomination. In fact, it is not only a common denominational belief, but in it all is a greater vision than ever before for an essential unity of all Christian churches to present a common spiritual goal for all mankind. So many of the old denominational prejudices have rightly died in the dust where they belong.

It is indeed an age when all men and women of spiritual goodwill must stand together completely integrated in Christ through love, tolerance and understanding, and lift their vision and work with the Lord to make the whole world free.

Inter-denominational work and fellowship is one of the paramount needs in the entire Christian field. It is so good to realise how this kind of work is increasing everywhere and how many organisations, like the one I serve, have sprung into being to help bridge that gap and share with all their basic experiences of love and faith in action.

What an astonishing faculty we have in memory! I paused for a few moments as I wrote the last words of the preceding paragraph, and was suddenly transported in memory across the ocean to sunny California. In a few seconds I was driving over the Golden Gate bridge with a mantle of fog swirling about its high towers, and on into the traffic-crowded streets of San Francisco. A few seconds more and I was in a Camp Farthest Out at Boulder Creek in the Santa Cruz mountains. And now I want to tell you something about these experiences.

As part of a three months' mission in the United States and Canada, I had been invited to share the leadership in three Camps Farthest Out. This is one of the vital world-wide witnessing movements based on love, service, and inter-denominational fellowship united by a common love for the Lord Jesus Christ. The name "Camp Farthest Out" means going farthest out with Christ for others at all times.

In all natural simplicity, groups of people meet together for a week of retreat and fellowship. There is no membership or organisation, apart from the necessary arranging of facilities for the many retreats which are held in the United States, Canada, England, India, Australia, New Zealand and many other places throughout the world.

This movement, and the United Prayer Tower in Minneapolis, was founded by the late Glenn Clark, that great man of prayer and spiritual vision whose life has been a true benediction to this age. He, with many others—an ever-growing army of leaders and helpers—has brought new life and new vision to countless thousands of people meeting in these retreats with Christ. And this inter-denominational scene is illumined by the Order of St. Luke, founded by the late John Gaynor Banks, and their international journal of Christian healing called *Sharing*.

I attended the first C.F.O. launched in England years ago by Glenn Clark and the Rev. and Mrs. Roland Brown at Swanwick. I was deeply moved and impressed by the spontaneity and joy of so many people spending a whole week together entirely in the Kingdom of God. Inevitably, everyone was quickened by the Holy Spirit and I received a great spiritual impetus there for my own work.

It was an inspiring experience to be with Glenn Clark in prayer. He was a man of absolute love and simplicity. When praying, he spoke as simply and conversationally to the Lord as he would to you or me. "Lord," he would say, "Mrs. Smith is in trouble and in pain. Will you please look after her? Thank you, Jesus—I leave her with you. Amen."

And I doubt if any man in modern times has had so many prayers completely answered as Glenn Clark.

So, on this particular mission, I spent a week in each of the Camps Farthest Out at Boulder Creek, Northern California; the Pennsylvania (Poconos Mountains) Camp and at Lake Murray Lodge, Ardmore, Oklahoma.

At Boulder Creek, the scattered cabins, communal dining-room and hall, nestled in a clearing in the redwood forest. These ancient trees raise their heads sometimes hundreds of feet towards the sky. Some were standing when Jesus walked in the Holy Land, and 350 people from far and wide had assembled to spend a week with God in this deep stillness of the forest.

There is nothing more stimulating than spiritual fellowship when everyone has a single-minded purpose of absolute dedication. These hundreds of men, women, teenagers and even little children, were here only to seek God's Will and His Love to open in them greater ways of service when they returned to their communities and churches.

It is easy to find God's Presence in such inspired company. There was no difficulty, whenever they were led in prayer or teaching, in finding the love that consummates any spiritual gathering, for the Spirit of the Lord was upon us all, and He was doing all the work for every one of us.

The Council Ring—just an inner group of people concerned with organisation—simply prayed their way daily through every need. And the efficiency of this kind of Divine Organisation in this, and in every C.F.O., is quite startling.

Some of my most inspired moments were with the youth attending this Camp. One day they "ganged up" and invited me to go for a hike into the mountains in the late evening. As we sang, tramped and frolicked up the dark and dusty road, closely hemmed in by the tall redwoods, I felt like a young boy of seventeen again! Flashlights twinkled or cast eerie lights into the shadows of the forest; lusty voices of girls and boys awakened watchdogs guarding isolated cottages somewhere amongst the trees; joy—just happy youth out on an adventure.

On the way home we all squatted under the trees and, as I talked and prayed with them, I knew that young people, on fire with the Holy Spirit as they were, would some day lead the whole world back to safety and sanity. How quickly these youngsters break through the musty cobwebs of prejudice and false restriction! How eagerly they embrace the simple truth when it is shown to them!

It was one of the greatest privileges of my life to allow them to clear some of the cobwebs clinging to me by their clean, fresh spirit and spontaneous friendship. And how young we can become ourselves when we dare to let ourselves go all the way with them.

All Americans seem to hurtle everywhere in huge cars, so the campus car park was always crowded as at any sports arena in England. So the boys and girls had a brilliant idea and set about washing and polishing all the cars with the zeal of an army of ants. I forget the amount of offerings, but it was some hundreds of dollars (doubled by a handsome cheque from a happy lady in the Camp), which was all given to the C.F.O. Scholarship Fund, which makes it possible for people without means to attend retreats free of charge.

What a wonderful world is in the making! And when all the boundless energy and interest of youth become harnessed to the boundless love of God, then wars, sin and sickness will vanish, and the Kingdom of the Lord will be established in the hearts and minds of men and women, as He desires it to be. And we shall all be boys and girls again, full of joy, enthusiasm and creativeness.

Christian Youth Movements are springing into being all over the world. Within the churches this is one of the surest signs heralding the new vision which is capturing the imagination of both clergy and laity in every denomination. In these days of high scientific development, what an opportunity we have now to reveal to the youth of every community the far-reaching significance of spiritual laws and the power of prayer!

Young folk, once they realise this truth, can enter into research and practice with even more enthusiasm and energy than they now give to their studies and new careers. They will see that all other aspects of creativeness and progression will yield infinitely greater fruits if they are centred in God, learning how to bring His Will and infinite strength to bear upon every objective in life.

And when we all recapture our eternal youth in Christ we shall lose our rigid ideas and musty prejudices and become once more flexible. In the Christian field of service especially do we need to be healed of the intolerance and distrust so often introduced, as we judge the motives and work of others who serve the Lord in patterns different from our own. Then we can become truly united in Christ and, instead of blocking the work of others who serve the Lord, we shall eagerly encourage them to fulfilment through ever greater love, dedication and fellowship.

I bring all this into perspective here because in the general picture of revival, of new vision to match the needs of this restless generation, it is good to realise that, in spite of the dangers and potential disasters of this time, a tremendous surge forward is taking place in countless ways.

I quote the Camps Farthest Out only as an example of so much intensified spiritual work being done everywhere. The Spirit quickens leaders and laity alike when, individually and collectively, they recognise the significance and urgency of the surrendered life.

It is the Father Who calls men and women to His Service. Their names are legion in every land.

Behind the leaders of the New Age, too numerous to mention, are all the millions who serve in the centre of every community. There are the ministers in every church, their Youth Group leaders and Sunday School teachers, and even the little lady who places flowers on the altar, nurses and kitchen staffs in hospitals, welfare workers and people who pray. The mother in a family is as much a part of the Divine Awakening as the most notable preacher on earth.

The simple fact is that we are all equal in God's sight, and each member of God's family has a vital part to take in the ever-awakening Light that shines for mankind. The list is endless, but we can be sure that the Good in man far outweighs the evil, and that more and more souls are being won to the Christ standard every day.

Inspiring and necessary though it is to be helped and guided by those who have had rich experiences in the spiritual way, it is still always true that the humblest among us can often be the channel of the greater works. Whenever and wherever the Lord reveals Himself, then beauty, good deeds and much love abound. The greatest miracle of all is that everyone, irrespective of race, colour, creed or religion, can always come home to the Father whenever they care to do so.

Very often simple and humble people can, like children, show us the way back to the Lord far more effectively than those who stumble over the hurdles of intellectual theology and analysis. The simple faith is prepared to leap over every fence of doubt or lack of understanding, and leave the issue completely in the care of a Father Who knows everything. The greater works, therefore, follow this simplicity of complete committal.

This reminds me of a friend I met in Toronto. He is a coloured man who was a guest, with his wife, in the home where I was staying. What a Christ-dedicated soul he is! This brother is a "Red-Cap", a porter, in the Grand Central Station in New York. And this station is his Cathedral.

I tape-recorded a talk with him. Listen inwardly to Mr. Ralston Young, Red-Cap 42, the disciple who has his church in a railway coach on Track 13!

"Well, I'm a 'Red-Cap' at Grand Central Terminal. They call us 'Red-Caps' because we wear red hats as we wait on the public, the travelling public, carrying their bags.

"About sixteen years ago I came to the full realisation that a Christian ought to be able to bring people to the Throne of Forgiveness in righteousness. So that sixteen years ago I joined a man who operates an elevator in the Greybar building, and with Christ in our lives we started a group in a dark railroad coach. Three times a week— Mondays, Wednesdays and Fridays at 12 o'clock—you'll find me in my uniform outside the gate where we assemble. Finally, we go down to this dark railroad coach. A lot of things happen on Track 13.

"Our purpose is really to give people the opportunity of knowing what the Christian Church stands for. There are so many in the city of New York, just like any other place, who have no church home and do not know anything about

Christianity. So on Track 13 they can listen to what Christians have to say in regard to meeting their Lord and Saviour Jesus Christ."

I asked Mr. Young what led him to begin this work. He replied:

"Well, I wasn't satisfied with just going to church on Sundays, and the Lord spoke to my heart and told me that I ought not to be ashamed or resentful of carrying bags. Before I met Christ I was miserable. I thought that the Red-Cap's job was too burdensome. It carried a stigma to be a Red-Cap. But after I found Christ, I discovered that I had a wonderful job. Then I was not only carrying a person's bag, but carrying the things that they cannot get into their bags, such as their sorrows, their griefs, their heartaches and their disappointments. So in Christ I began to be creative, and helped people to come into this dark railroad coach to talk about their problems and release them to the Lord.

"Once I counted 39 people in the coach. But even if I am the only person there at noontime, the Lord has laid it on my heart to be steadfast and present, so that if anyone comes, there will be Christian fellowship on Track 13. I remember, for example, about ten years ago, a young man with an important job came down to see what we had on Track 13. When he had been about four times he said, 'You know, I did not realise that I was such a mug. And now,' he said, 'that has to stop.' And so he went back to his church and organised a Sunday School class.

"He taught Sunday School, and finally he became the superintendent. About four years after that he said, 'I've got to go into the Ministry. I cannot avoid it.' 'I've been tussling with this thing,' he said, 'but the Lord wants me in the Ministry.' Well, he left his job, sold his home, and went into a seminary. We went to his ordination. Finally he went to Florida, and built a new Church home. And he said, 'It's through a dark railroad coach, having fellowship with people in Christ, that I got this wonderful revelation from God to enter His Ministry.' "

Then my friend continued:

"Before I met Christ—which I call B.C. in my life—I was just interested in looking at the clock. But now it's different. It's really helping people, not only carrying their bags but being interested in them, sensitive to their needs and their desires. And so often, God has laid it on my heart to say something helpful, to be kind or go the extra mile. As I walk the concourse, I say within myself, 'Father, I'm so thankful to You that I AM a Red-Cap.'

"The officials have never given me the 'green light' about our railroad coach. But one of them came down and said, 'Ralston, in my office every Monday and Wednesday and Friday I pray and ask God to help you fellows on Track 13.' "

Who is the greatest amongst us? None—for only God is Good. As long as His Goodness shines in any life, all is well. When it shines as brightly as it does in the service of Red-Cap 42, there is a Light to inspire every minister and every layman to express the greater works of God. We can reveal Him just where we are.

This, as always, is the Light of the New Age and it can only dispel the darkness as quickly as we personally arise in Christ to allow His Light to shine through us in service, one by one, until we are all filled with it.

"Behold, I make all things new!" The world is already deeply involved in this Divine Awakening, because the Father works to make it so. I flew home to England inspired and more dedicated than ever through the Christ Love I found in so many people in the New World.

*　　　*　　　*　　　*

Father, help us to be humble, simple in our trust, and loving enough to be Thy Light to all whom You send into our daily experience. May we be so centred in Thee that we may behold the Christ in everyone else, and thus give our lives in Thy Service, showing by our example of prayer, thought, word and deed the true brotherhood of man as it is in Heaven, through Jesus Christ, our Lord. Amen.

4

The Valley of a Thousand Hills

I will lift up mine eyes unto the hills, from whence cometh my help.

PSALM 121 : 1.

THE BEAUTIFUL ISLANDS of Britain, spilling over with a population of over fifty-two million people, still stand as a citadel of freedom for the world. Every culture or civilisation rises through the mistakes, successes and experiences of its people over long periods of time. And, whatever else, these island tribes have a history unique in world-wide adventures and organisation on the one hand, and on the other of creative ingenuity in their hitherto sea-bound isolation.

Like individuals, nations too have their special personalities and gifts of creativeness. Even as men and women in a community share and express the national life, so does each country or continent form part of a perfect pattern ultimately to be woven into the fabric of the whole.

Therefore, the wise man of this generation will always work to that end, eager to recognise the virtues and values inherent in the peoples of every land, equally ready to be compassionate, understanding and tolerant with their traditions, mistakes or weaknesses which do not square with his own outlook and experience.

The world traveller increasingly begins to comprehend the national characteristics and aspirations of both the advanced nations abroad, and those as yet backward in their evolution.

There is an urgent yearning everywhere to find enduring solutions to intolerable world problems, as more and more nations struggle for freedom or prosperity, and often for domination over others.

However inadequate, as yet, may be our approach to the comprehensive solution of international problems, it is true that nations like the United States and the British Commonwealth of Nations are united in a common vision of freedom for all mankind, and millions have died in the holocausts of war trying to uphold it by that means.

Even though enduring peace and progression can never be secured through wholesale slaughter and destruction, nor by the stockpiling and threat of atomic missiles, it is still true that the motivating intention has been a search for freedom and peace for all.

In these battered islands of Britain during the last war, conservative Englishmen demonstrated, perhaps as never before in world history, how strong is the human spirit in determination and endurance when it believes in some great ideal. And, while everyone, everywhere, hates warfare and all that it means, countless men and women of ordinary family homes gave their all, including life, rather than submit to tyranny.

The evolutionary awakening still moves inevitably towards predestined fulfilment. In spite of the gravity of world conflicts, crystallised clearly to our general view in the East-West Communism versus the rest, and the blood-letting wound in the side of all nations through massive armaments, thinkers everywhere are for the first time seriously awakening to the need for absolute peace based on equality, justice and mutual help.

We are gradually gaining a new vision about the real needs of lesser nations. The United States and Britain pour out unselfish help in countless ways, from finance to educational facilities, to people in need all over the world. While much of this may still be motivated by fear, seeking to gather adherents to our side and to make them strong, the basic instinct is a true world communion in freedom.

While dangers abound on every side, this is no time for despair or despondency. We are living in the greatest age in the long history of man on earth. And it brings with it the richest opportunity yet known to open the way to the spiritual, mental and material prosperity which has ever been the true goal and heritage of man from the beginning.

By the very force of the law of cause and effect, war has long since ceased to be a profitable or effective solution. We are in a state of stalemate. The final clash of inter-continental missiles with atomic warheads can only liquidate all humanity, so a general or even a child comes to the inevitable conclusion that we are reaching the end of this chapter of human experience.

Although we still stand embattled, our arms are as useless as wooden muskets. Common sense, inspired by the awakening vision, will infallibly lead us into a position when we can gladly throw these useless toys away. We shall then concentrate all our resources on the creative arts, which are so much more exciting and true to the inward genius of the individual and nation.

Long neglected in the full expression of its potential, the spiritual truth now comes shining back into the minds of millions of people. The teaching of Jesus Christ, and its essential essence of scientific reality, is being more clearly understood today than since the days of His Life and Ministry. In the beginning, the peoples of the early Church were motivated by a blind and simple faith. Today, while the need for simplicity still remains, we can embrace the full Gospel of Jesus with a faith backed by all the accumulated findings of science and an educated reason and understanding.

So far as world problems are concerned, it is a startling fact that no nation on earth has yet realised, or sought, fully to implement the simplest of all truths and solutions. Yet even a boy at school can see that war, for example, is the product of hate, fear or selfishness, in all its manifold degrees of expression. And that these qualities in human nature, whether expressed by individual or nation, are contrary to the Law of Love which Jesus preached as the absolute Commandment.

It is but a short step to realise, therefore, that the problems, sickness, sin and strife of man or country are essentially spiritual problems which can only be solved by the application of spiritual principles.

Thoughts, ideas, beliefs are living things and they produce of their kind. It is the inexorable law that as a man (or nation) thinks, so he is, and he creates his experience accordingly. The subjection of weaker people brings a corresponding reaction in countless ways, often not reaching finality for many generations. The Law of Cause and Effect cannot be bypassed—except by Love, which can transmute past cause and release the new cause, leading to perfect awakening and fulfilment.

Every bomb dropped on "victor" or "defeated" alike represents the living negative thoughts behind their projection and, inevitably, we get caught in the racing storms of action and reaction, ever multiplying in potency as ideas concerning conflict grow. The proof of this profound law is clearly shown in the evolution of war from pointed spears to mass bombing and atomic weapons—linked with the expanded ideas about how to use them on a world scale.

There never was, and never will be, the possibility of a war to end war. Such an approach could only end, inevitably, in world suicide, by the very nature of the laws which govern the world and the laws of mind which must project what is thought into outward manifestation.

But today, the ever-awakening mind of man is beginning to recognise this obvious truth. We all know, without any preaching, that our real need is for peace on earth and an opportunity to enjoy an abundant, creative and prosperous life. And, because we can recognise the potentials of the true solution, of course we shall increasingly devote our vision, integrity and inborn spiritual instinct to bring forth the new ideas and beliefs to produce the answers we so sorely need.

We are considering, of course, the evolutionary awakening that is coming into being. We are still only on the threshold of this new Christ Age. We may still have to pass through many fires to distil the pure truth in the form accepted as basic principle from which none will wish to deviate.

Like education, it quickens when the need is known and as minds produce the vision, ideas and dedication always necessary when fundamental issues are at stake.

Be thankful, then, that you live at this time of the Divine Awakening. It is the greatest honour God could ever have bestowed upon you. It is the time in history crucial to all the ages yet to be, and you, inevitably, have your particular and unique place in this Divine Pattern if you will only take it.

In the light of modern knowledge about creation, life, the mind and the revealed confirmation of Jesus Christ, every man, woman and child is brimming over with potential for tremendous spiritual experience, adventure and service.

For too long we have left the greater works to the spiritually illumined ones who have always tried to blaze this trail for humanity. We have hidden our greatest gifts behind a wall of belief in our own unworthiness, inadequacy or limitation, leaving the real works in the hands of ministers or people whose vocation it is to serve the community spiritually.

The simple truth is, and always will be, that everyone is equal in God, and that everyone has a unique and wonderful contribution to make which none other can do. We may praise the Lord and eternally give thanks to His Love and Wisdom, that He made it possible for everyone, saint or sinner, rich or poor, master or under-privileged, to become a Light unto the world.

There are about three thousand million souls on earth. And there is only one you! What the entire family is expressing as world consciousness, inevitably includes every thought that has crossed your mind since you were born. This rule applies to a nation, your city, home and personality. It represents a revelation of responsibility and potential which none can escape and which all should eagerly embrace.

Many of the most powerful works for good on earth have come through simple, humble people. And many of our disasters have come from erroneous ideas born in great intellects, backed by the power of finance and other powerful material-istic minds, united in implementing their desires.

So the inspiration and vision for this day and age is the vital importance of the individual and his recognition of the infinite possibilities that lie within his reach and range, when he opens his life and mind to the ever-present, directive power of God. There is no limit to what can be accomplished, apart from the limitations we fix upon ourselves.

Faith, fixed round any idea, will move towards its goal, if linked steadfastly with love, imagination, will, and dedi-cated purpose to stay the course right through to fulfilment.

Faith, fixed on the Father and wedded to infinite potential and objectives, will also allow Him to produce experience on a Divine level where there are no limits or limitations whatso-ever.

The Gospel was written for you. It is your truth according to the degree you believe it and take it through into your exper-ience. But it is a whole Truth, and can only be known when we become prepared to embrace the whole of it as a way of life.

Faith, for example, without love is as useless as tinsel when you need gold. Love without faith, good though it is, still crowds out the greater Light by the clouds of limitation, fear or doubt. It is a full Gospel which only becomes Good News when we are willing to behold the significance of total sur-render, the dedicated life, and the practice of the Presence of God in love, with a fearless faith matching the power with which He seeks to endow us.

God, and the world, need you. Christ is looking for you as a disciple who is willing to allow Him to use you to fulfil a particular pattern which HE planted in you when He gave you the gift of life. What amazing experiences lie in wait for us all, once we grasp the all-pervading fact that it is the Father Who opens the way for us!

There is no haphazard planning in His Spirit. While it is true we have a profound measure of free will within which to unfold our own personalities, it is still true that we dwell in the midst of a Perfection Pattern and Principle to which, in the end, we shall all conform and awaken. It is our nature and joy to do so, and when we tire of pains and problems, fear and frustration, and lack of peace, we will gladly let these lesser things fall away and enter into our eternal purpose.

There is a law, therefore, that we are experiencing the things our souls need for their growth. Sin leads ultimately to redemption. Sickness, in the eternal sense, leads to health and well-being. Sadness is the threshold of joy. The Cross of Christ was the herald of Resurrection, and still is for all of us.

The simple fact that you are reading these words means that, in ways perhaps unknown to you or me, there is something here which you are ready to receive. God never makes a mistake, and His influence is always for our highest good. These words are necessary for you, not because I am writing them, but because your life swings in the orbit of Divine Spirit, and it is the Father's work to ensure that whatever we need at any time shall reach us when we are ready to accept it.

You are more important to God than you are to yourself. And this brings to mind some more thrilling experiences I had in South Africa.

*　　*　　*　　*

As our plane flew away from the airport at Nice, en route for South Africa, I thought we were bound for an overnight stop at Cairo. In mid-afternoon we flew in to the Land of the Nile and across horizon-wide desert with an occasional glimpse of the strip of vegetation beside the river which has produced all the corn of Egypt from time so remote that little record remains.

And we landed at the dusty military airport of Luxor on the Upper Nile! I was overjoyed because for years I had longed for the opportunity to visit the ancient birthplace of Egyptian kings, temples and tombs. This was Old Testament country indeed, with pictures of Moses and the tribes of Israel already quickening my imagination!

The strip of desert was fringed on one side by the cream

coloured airport building wearing what to me was as good as a crown, a bold sign "Luxor Airport" with a few squiggles of Egyptian underneath it. As we disembarked, the sun was just setting like a ball of molten gold set in a deep blue sky, and palm trees stood like still sentinels on the edge of interminable sand. A few Egyptian soldiers carefully watched our progress into the customs, and we were soon engulfed in the tide of strange language and people.

A plane-load of elegant Indian ladies, dressed in pure white saris, were waiting to fly through the skies to some Mecca of their spiritual dreams. The little mark painted over the "third eye" on the forehead of each somehow enhanced their beauty and aspiration, and I wished them well in a little silent prayer.

In a strange, inward way, it was like coming home. This feeling grew as a battered old bus churned up the thick dust on the road into Luxor, and appeared to scatter from its path a constant stream of children, old men on donkeys with loads of produce, and burnoused Arabs trudging home to their adobe shacks. Although a "civilised" engine was carrying us, the scene along the road, the camels and donkeys, the flowing robes of men and women, the bare feet, dust and flies, offered no change whatsoever from the scenes described to us in Biblical times.

It was all so true to my imagination. I was back in the time when the Pharaohs ruled and Egypt was the land of the great. In spite of the dust and evident squalor around these outskirts of the town, it was exciting and refreshing, as though I needed to assuage some hidden hunger to know more of the people of long ago.

We were taken to a large hotel on the banks of the Nile, right alongside the towering columns of a ruined temple. And I marvelled again at the magnificent architecture those ancient Egyptians conceived and created.

After dinner, the airline organised a party to visit the age-old Temple of Amen-Ra. We went like a cavalcade crowded into a dozen horse-drawn cabs, which might well have graced the streets of fashionable London in the nineteenth century.

In the full moonlight, no breeze and a clear sky, we jogged for several dusty miles towards our temple. The stream of children, closely robed men and women, donkeys and camels never ceased, and one wondered where they could all be going. In the dim light they looked almost eerie in their gowns, and we were followed by strange calls and cackling laughter.

The Temple of Amen-Ra. I was really excited by the time we reached the great portals. Here in the open the moonlight bathed these many acres of columns and ruins with a mystic halo. It was not difficult to flow back down the ages to feel something of the ceremonial, power and panoply of ancient courts and kings.

As I walked through the huge portals giving entry to the temple, something jogged the memory that Moses himself used to pass through these gates. It was a heart-quickening thought. This place was planted in antiquity five, or even six thousand years ago, and so much of it is still standing in mute witness to the days of a great civilisation.

Wanting to capture more of the real nature of this scene, I let the party drift away with the guide, and wandered through the stillness and dust of distant days. Cleopatra's Needle (as we call it) came from this temple, and today stands proclaiming the ancient glory of Egypt on the Thames Embankment in London.

This came to my mind as I saw "Cleopatra's other needle" lying in the temple precincts. I guessed it to be seventy feet long, cut out of one block of granite, and found it covered with hieroglyphs. Many of the still standing walls portrayed in the old Egyptian picture-writing the adventures of kings and queens, priests and warriors, hunters and slaves.

The moonlight transformed everything, of course. The harsh glare of the noonday sun might only have emphasised the ruins, dust and rubble. But the moonlight transported me to an enchanted land, and I was thrilled by the mystical atmosphere created by the magnificent visible expression of an ancient barbarous people.

Turning a corner, I was startled to see a beautiful woman

in stone, twenty feet high, sitting on a throne. She had calmly disregarded time for five thousand years. A queen? A priestess?

But far away, in another valley, the Valley of the Kings, perhaps her mummy still rests somewhere among the tombs of the pomp and pageantry of man's early days.

We all have our roots in this dust, and should humbly remember that, even as we represent the total product of man's thinking and corresponding action through the ages, so do we influence every event today, and provide the springboard from which our race will leap, or fall, in the future.

The Pharaohs of old would have marvelled indeed could they have seen our great air-liner soaring up into the golden dawn next morning! The heat-seared tracks across hundreds of miles of desert must have presented formidable problems to the camel caravans of those days. Yet born of the same mentality which created majestic temples and tombs in Egypt, man's insatiable urge to create and conquer today speeds him effortlessly on wings above it all.

So along the Nile, across the deserts, over central African jungles, seventy people swept through the skyways sleeping, eating, reading, safely and at ease. The captain of our modern chariot wiggled its wings as we went over the equator and the Livingstone country.

And the occasional clusters of native kraals seemed mutely to remind us that darkest Africa is still a child in the human family, needing so much love, care and help from her elder brothers.

The evening lights of Johannesburg and the Jan Smuts airport welcomed us into South Africa. Even travellers by plane grow weary and it was good to be on the ground again.

Johannesburg is built on a mountain of gold, and surrounded by hills of yellow refuse spewed up from the endless tunnels where many men have burrowed, like beavers, for the treasure which is so often the god before whose throne we worship. Nevertheless, it is a great city, and as modern as any New York or Pittsburgh, and just as busy. Next morning found me in the air again, bound for East London where my present mission was to begin.

*   *   *   *

The purpose of this writing now is not to go step by step outlining the details of a Divine healing mission through the great cities of sunny South Africa, but to point, by example and incident, to the power of Christ in simple people when the Lord takes over. I reiterate, with all emphasis, that the whole world will arise to new dimensions of love, faith, prayer and creativeness when people in any or every vocation realise what can be done when they fully awaken to the power of the spirit.

Mr. and Mrs. Gordon-Davis, who founded the Grace Dieu Healing Sanctuary in East London, are people like that. They met me, as a brother in Christ, at the airport, and took me into their hearts and home. It is always good to see a spiritual work in being. But always behind the accomplished fact lies the hidden struggle, endless hours of prayer and practice, sacrifice of material possessions, disciplines and a way of faith which can only discover its potential by going forward, following some vision, with perfect trust.

But all things have their beginning and in their case, too, there had to be the completeness of giving, loving and faith before the Lord could take two simple people to set them on to the road of service in the public weal. It is this which always stirs my imagination, because I know full well the yearnings, courage and first steps which such an enterprise involves. The present sanctuary stands as a monument to all those hidden moments only known in the sacred recesses of their minds—and to God. And it was the Father Who did the work corresponding to them.

When they came to know of our work in England, Mrs. Gordon-Davis was even inspired to make a special trip to England to investigate the possibilities of missions in South Africa. That kind of faith and sacrifice *cannot* fail to move mountains.

Since then, my visits to Africa have been organised by these two Christian workers. With no experience of such organisation, they have simply prayed their way through every situation, with the result that the Lord led us into mutual service in churches of most denominations in that country.

Travelling on these missions has been a happy time of fellowship and service, and through them it has been possible to see the vision of Christ's Light ever shining into all the darkness of that continent. All this because two people completely handed their lives over to the Lord.

It was on one such mission that we eventually arrived at Durban for services arranged by a prayer group there. It is in these parts that the Rev. Edward Winckley has the Kearsney Healing Home and the Prayer Healing Fellowship. We travelled the 400 miles from East London to Durban by car. It took us through the Transkei, through the territories which are reserved for Africans. It was very interesting to see their dwelling places on these green hills which flow right up to the mountains in the distance. These people must have lived there for many hundreds of years. Their round adobe huts, with thatched cone-shaped roofs, looked like a scattering of giant mushrooms across the veldt.

The African sometimes has two or three wives. Each wife lives in a separate kraal, but the first wife becomes the mistress of the whole household. His wealth is judged by the number of cattle he owns and, in consequence, the pastures looked very much overgrazed by the large numbers of scrawny-looking animals. How great is their need for every aspect of civilisation, judged by western standards!

In startling contrast, Durban is an exciting ultra-modern city set in sub-tropical splendour. The kraals in the hills and the thriving city on the coast seemed to crystallise so vividly the story of man's beginnings and progress through the thousands of years of his awakening.

We went up into the Valley of a Thousand Hills, about an hour's journey from Durban, to see that great man, Mr.

Don Mackenzie, who founded the famous Toc H Settlement there to care for crippled and tubercular Africans.

This settlement in the Valley of a Thousand Hills, on the boundary of the African Reserves, is like the arms of Christ extended in compassion to rescue these under-privileged sick brothers. It is now a well-established hospital with all kinds of additional activities such as general education, arts and crafts, rehabilitation centres, and technical methods which this man of genius has developed down the years to teach and help the African to take a useful and happy place in the community.

I had been invited to conduct a service in their beautiful church. As I prayed and felt Christ's Presence among this dedicated congregation of African children and adults, I could not help realising that Jesus Himself moved among simple people like these in the hills of the Holy Land. I was quickened by their singing. The spontaneous and melodious rhythms throbbed with the mystic voice of Africa, with an inner power which must inevitably lead them to fulfil the destiny the Father has prepared for these people.

After the service Mr. Mackenzie went across to the organ. The church was now empty, except for our party. As he played, I thought of other great pioneers in this continent; people like Dr. Albert Schweitzer, in central Africa, Livingstone, the hundreds of missionaries, and so many who have given their lives to advance the well-being of the natives.

I asked Don Mackenzie to tell the story of his work, and was privileged to record his words which I wish now to share with you. This is what he said:

"Every night, standing on the verandah of our home, we listen to the cry of people across the valley, and this is specially poignant on a summer's evening. And I ask myself what brought us here, what gave us this happiness? So I think back on those years, and I believe it all really started out on the Western Desert in the war years, when we felt that we would like to give something back—if we could be spared to come back. Then when we came back there was that terrible feeling of inadequacy, a feeling that we were out of tune with life. And so I began to feel somehow or other that I should do something in this great need among our under-privileged people in South Africa.

"I began to pray for the first time for a long time. I felt that I had been out of tune with God, and so I began to pray. The more I thought of these things, the more I began to feel that I had a duty to put something back.

"I can't tell you, you know, how much I struggled. I wriggled and struggled, and could think of ninety-nine good reasons why *I* should not do these things, but could think of a lot of good reasons why everybody else should! And then it seemed to me that our people, privileged Europeans, owed them a great debt—a debt of gratitude if you like. The whole of the happiness and prosperity of our country had been built upon their labours and endeavours.

"And so, thinking on these things, I used to go to church, and sitting at the very back I wondered how God could use me, a very ordinary man. And you know, one day, with an absolute certainty—and this I cannot explain to anybody—I just *knew* the finger of God had lightly touched me on the shoulder. I knew that with all my limitations, with all my inadequacies, all the restrictions that I had placed upon myself, there was a job of work I had to go and do for God.

"And so I began. In the name of Toc H, I resigned my career. I collected around me a band of young fellows and girls to help me, and set out in an old wagon and eventually arrived in this great valley where we had been able to lease a piece of ground. I set up camp here and was alone—the others returned. I can't tell you of the dreadful, enormous loneliness of those first days—it was tremendous. It was the first time, you know, that I had felt the security of insecurity, if I can put it that way. I felt for the first time in my life that I was able to walk with God. I felt for the first time in my life that I knew the meaning of that little poem 'Put your hands into the hands of God, and that shall be safer than a known way'.

"In the mornings I used to look out over these tremendous hills, and used to feel then, in the words of the Psalmist, that I had to lift up mine eyes unto the hills from whence cometh my help, because I knew that no help would come from anywhere else.

"And so the days went by in a tremendous sense of security. Very little food to eat, and no money whatsoever, since we'd sold everything we possessed. Day by day went by, and then the time came when I built our first huts. I had no money whatsoever. Then somebody said that we could not build on land which was leased.

"Well, I thought that something had to be done about this new challenge. It was a wet, miserable Saturday night. There was no one about, and the only movement came from a burning candle. And as I was thinking about this new development I had a tremendous urge to pray—I, who had so rarely prayed before. I had this tremendous urge. I got on my knees and I handed the whole job over to God. I felt God had got me here and therefore would never let me down. In the language of a very famous man I said, 'Give me the tools, and we will try and do the job.' I felt better because of that.

"I will always remember, because I wrote it down in my diary. There was a little candle burning, and I remembered those wonderful words of Confucius. Remember them? 'It is better to light one small candle than to curse the darkness.' Well, I thought of that. The next day the rain poured, but I walked up the long valley until I got to the village where there was a letter. And the letter was signed by 'The Old Policeman'. It was very terse and to the point. It said, 'Do you know what you are doing? And if you do, do you own the ground you're on? And if you don't, have you an option of purchase? And if you have, how much is it?' I just sat down and I replied, 'Dear Old Policeman', and then I told him what I have told you.

"The bank manager wrote to me about a week later and said that the whole sum of money necessary for the purchase of this ground had been paid to the credit of an account. All I had to do was to give an undertaking that we would purchase the ground.

"I've still got that letter. When I saw it I just knew that, somehow or other, a miracle had happened again, and that God was helping us here. I really did. And so we set to work.

"My old friend, Alan Paton, came to my assistance, and after writing the book *Cry, The Beloved Country* he donated the whole of the proceeds of the world film première in town. That was terrific. It brought me in, for the first time, some money which enabled us to carry on with our work.

"So the great day came in 1952, nearly eighteen months later, when we were able to take in our first patients. It was a tremendous experience that, to see the fruits of eighteen months of terrific hard work. And so these youngsters came in. We never slept a wink all night worrying about them. It was just because it was all so new.

"Then a wonderful woman came out from England to help me as matron. And so we began to build up our medical work.

"But here, you know, I want to tell you something. That though I regard the work with tuberculosis as fundamental—that's what we're here for—there is another work which I think we are doing, and must always do, and that is to build those—how can I explain it to you?—those little pockets of reconciliation which become like brightly lighted little islands in a sea of bewilderment in South Africa.

"As time went on we gradually built the place up. When I look around it now and see how it has grown, I'm filled with a wonder that is beyond all expression. I know that ordinary people like me could never have done this job alone, and I know that God has used some very wonderful

c

people to come along and help us in everything we've ever done.

"Here I would just like to say that one evening we were walking in the streets of Durban, and I saw a young boy—crippled and very, very badly paralysed—begging. A lady came along and put a shilling into his hand. I said to my wife, 'You see, that's what we do in South Africa. We buy our conscience for a shilling.' It's terribly bad, and it's bad for a youngster to receive something for nothing, to capitalise on his handicap. I went to see the Government about this, and they were really sympathetic. They told me to go ahead and build a hospital here for crippled boys, where they could be medically treated and receive training as well, so that they could learn a trade. I thought it was a wonderful idea.

"They would not give me any money until I had raised the initial sum when they would give me a pound for a pound. Once again I didn't know how to raise this money. So I did what anybody would have done. I went for a long walk in the grass with my dog. I walked and talked with God. You know, it came as an astounding thing to me again—out of somewhere this great wonderful feeling—not to be afraid, not to worry about a thing. But to follow any lead that would come. *Any* lead—just follow it!

"Well, the lead came, and it came not from the Gentile but from the Jew. The Jews invited me to come and speak at their annual meeting, which I did. I will always remember saying to them, 'It seems to me a wonderful thing that a Gentile can speak to a Jew on a matter of compassion and pity and sympathy'. And they rose to the occasion magnificently. One young man said he had been looking for this for years, and could he give me £1,500 (U.S. $4,500) to begin with? Of course, I went straight to the Government and told them. Do you know what they said to me? They said, 'We just did that to get rid of you, and here you're back again!'

"Gradually, this place has been built up. A special school

for the handicapped has been built. Well, one side of the ward was built and the first batch of cripples arrived. I shall always remember them. They looked such a pitiful little group of people. They seemed to me like the flotsam and jetsam of life. And among them there was a young lad named Reuben. He was born a perfectly normal child, but developed T.B. in his spine and it paralysed him dreadfully. It curved his legs under his chin. His parents had taken him to a witch doctor but nothing happened. They took him to one of the big hospitals in Durban but they rejected him because he was a chronic case. They took him to a little mission hospital where they eventually took him in.

"He was covered in bedsores—he was in agony. One of the sisters told him in later years that he had looked like a little hunted animal. Well, five and a half years of devoted surgical and medical attention brought Reuben to the stage where his legs were straightened and put into calipers, and then we taught him how to walk. It took me three months of patient teaching.

"One day Reuben was walking round and he suddenly said to me, 'Old frog (that's the name they call me), I can walk.' You know, it was a most moving moment to see him swinging along on his crutches. And I said to him, 'Well, come and give thanks to Him to Whom your thanks are due.' So he went into the morning service—we always start the day with a little morning service.

"And here Reuben, lifting up his face and hanging on to his table, said in Zulu (which is a poetic language): 'I am a cripple, I am handicapped and I am not as you are. When I look about me and see so many boys and men who are crippled, I feel it is my duty to tell you it gives me peace. One day I was born, you know, and I knew nothing about it. One day I will die, and I will know nothing about that. But this I do know, that when I come face to face with my Creator, He will *not* say to me, "Reuben, you haven't brought your crutches. Reuben, you haven't brought your calipers. And you'll not walk around in the Heavenly places". Ah no," said Reuben, 'He will want me just as I am. And if that keeps *me* happy, surely it can keep *you* happy and at peace.' Well, I thought that was a lovely story.

"We have about two hundred and fifty people altogether. The majority are young children, with some fifty or sixty adults."

I asked Mr. Mackenzie, in the light of his vast experience, if he believed the Africans could be led fully to adopt the Christ Way of life and take their part in the civilisations of the world. He replied:

"I believe that is the only thing that will save Africa. I really believe it. They are most responsive. I want to say this to you. We have been here ten years, and we have never felt frustrated. In all that time we have felt that there has been a mutual respect, one for the other.

"We also continue their education. We have a little school. It really is lovely, you know, in the mornings. We have all the little disciplines which children need—they must have that. And that little school bell rings out each morning, you know, for these little people whose future is so uncertain—so uncertain and so unknown. And I think we can prepare them here—in a spiritual sense, we *can* prepare them. They have an economic struggle ahead of them too. Fundamentally, you see, the settlement does take care of the sick, and it does care for the maimed. But I repeat, I really do think the settlement here is breaking down these racial tensions by building up these basic things.

"Do you hear that bell ringing now? As I just said, that's the school bell which rings out every day.

"Well, perhaps now our lives here will be able to cast a little light into the darkness of many a little human abyss. And it might help to build a happy South Africa.

"I call these children our little 'shobbi shauvals', which

means little tadpoles—the little frogs. And you know what they call me—they call me the 'old frog'.

"I do want to thank you for coming up today. It was a great experience for them. You know, this is the first time they have ever received a blessing from a white man. That was a tremendous thing for them. And, you know, they wanted to remain behind after you left this morning, just to think and talk about it. I really want to thank you."

On the wall was a plaque. Mr. Mackenzie said it had been inscribed by a crippled African. It seemed so aptly to symbolise his work that I share it with you:

Did you see His outstretched hands
Nailed on Golgotha's hill?
To signify He loved all lands
Even the infidel.

Two thousand years since then have passed,
Twenty-four thousand moons.
Surely His message cannot last,
But fade as last year's tunes?

Yet, in the town at Botha's Hill
His joy and work prevails,
For healing hands attend the ill,
And Love replaces nails.

Thank You, Father, that Thy Love *is* the light of the Living Christ on this Golgotha's Hill in the Valley of a Thousand Hills, as Thy Love reaches all Thy people, everywhere, through Jesus Christ our Lord. May we likewise offer Thee the True talents of our love and faith, that we may be used to serve those who are weaker than ourselves, and to Bless all people we meet or know today.

* * * *

After some weeks travelling and conducting services in the great cities of South Africa, it was time to leave Johannesburg for London.

Thousands of miles north from the Valley of a Thousand

Hills, the plane touched down in Cairo airport for an over-night stop. The Nile flows through the centre of this seething city as calmly as the world speeds through space.

In the morning we had the opportunity of seeing the pyra-mids and the sphinx in the early sunshine. Again I caught a glimpse of man's indomitable spirit as he etched his ideas in the stones that reflect them down the ages.

The sphinx was old with unknown origins even in the days of the early Pharaohs, when it was reclaimed from the tides of sand. With Dr. Schweitzer, when we pause before such monu-ments, surely we can have a profound reverence for life?

But, marvelling before this magnificent architecture, I looked beyond the inscrutable face of the Sphinx of the Ages, and thought of the living work of a modern apostle, Don Mackenzie, among the children of this Africa today, among "the least of these", and knew that here was true greatness—for you, for me and for all.

> "Verily I say unto you, Inasmuch as ye have done it unto one of the least of these my brethren, ye have done it unto Me" (Matt. 25: 40).

I returned to England, a great citadel of freedom, and still found the same thread of salvation woven between all people. This Divine dynamic awakens the soul of an African even as it touches a church in London. It stirs equally in New York or New Zealand, and becomes blended in the minds of all people as they lift their vision to comprehend the essential unity of man throughout the world.

In the next chapter I would like to tell you how a Divine Illumination transformed my life and revealed this eternal truth of Christ's teaching.

* * *

Prayer of St. Francis for Africa.

Lord, make me a channel of Thy Peace
That where there is hatred—I may bring love,
That where there is wrong—I may bring the spirit of for-
giveness,

That where there is discord—I may bring harmony,
That where there is error—I may bring truth,
That where there is doubt—I may bring faith,
That where there is despair—I may bring hope,
That where there are shadows—I may bring Thy Light,
That where there is sadness—I may bring joy.

Lord, grant that I may seek rather
To comfort—than to be comforted;
To understand—than to be understood;
To love—than to be loved;

For it is by giving—that one receives;
It is by self-forgetting—that one finds;
It is by forgiving—that one is forgiven;
It is by dying—that one awakens to eternal life.

Amen.

5

The Light of the World

I am the light of the world: he that followeth me shall not walk in darkness, but shall have the light of life.

JOHN 8: 12.

THE VITAL DYNAMIC of Jesus lies in the fact that He is the Light of the World and the Salvation of men. "I and the Father are one" is the greatest statement ever made, because He then constantly releases and shares this truth with us all in ways which are fundamental, without exception, to every aspect of our own personal potential and possibility.

The word "salvation" is profound. When fully understood and expressed, it introduces the mind to a principle so transcendental that it awakens the tiny human life into one of intense love, joy, peace, power and ever-growing perfection. Salvation through Christ brings into personal experience the practical help and infinite love, wisdom, guidance and knowledge of God. Its potency for each person is infinite in scope and is always manifested in states of spiritual well-being. Christ brings the Light of Perfect Everything to mind, soul, body and the events which engage our attention day by day.

Salvation is the Light of Christ illuminating the infinite vista of our eternal nature, and quickening the vision of our real purpose here on earth by bringing our understanding of the truth of a continuous unfolding of personality and creative achievement on other planes hereafter.

Therefore, Jesus says, in His all-embracing instructions in the Sermon on the Mount. "Ye are the light of the World" (Matt. 5:14).

In the first chapter of St. John we are also given the truth of our identity in the Father. We have all read it many times, but consider now the significance and implication of these words, when we think of the possibility of God's Life being in us.

"In Him was life; and the life was the light of men.

"And the light shineth in darkness; and the darkness comprehended it not.

"There was a man sent from God, whose name *was* John.

"The same came for a witness, to bear witness of the Light, that *all men* through him might believe.

"He was not that Light, but *was sent* to bear witness of that Light.

"*That* was the true Light, which lighteth every man that cometh into the world."

Jesus Himself tells us that the Kingdom of God is within, which can only mean that our personal experience of communion with Him, and all it implies, must be an inward awareness. He says: "Neither shall they say, Lo here! or lo there! for, behold, the kingdom of God is within you" (Luke 17:21).

This was probably a strange doctrine to the people of those days, but now we can all realise its truth without much difficulty. Modern scientists in every field of research have been led into the inner recesses of matter. The doctor examines the physical cell in a body, but his attention is now drawn to the invisible properties of life, mind, and motivating laws which make the microscopic cell of blood, flesh or bone exist in its unique form and behaviour.

He becomes increasingly fascinated by the mysterious processes which create new cells and build them into the harmonious but highly complicated organism of the body, male and female. He wants to know the secrets of the genes, and the creative power which plans and executes the countless operations which produce a baby and a man. In a thousand ways, medical and psychological research become involved in seeking the secrets of the Power Within.

Even in "inert" matter like a stone or a grain of sand, the scientist of today no longer looks at the outward picture, but probes into the realm of energy, the atomic "emptiness" and the invisible Laws which motivate the surging but mathematically precise action within the tiniest speck of matter, or the composite whole of a world or universe. And he knows that this action is operative from *within*, and not from *without*.

When we consider the structure of a man, with his life, mind and body, we do not need to stretch our imaginations to grasp the significant and observable fact that everything we know about ourselves is an inward realisation. The mind itself functions invisibly within, and even though a large degree of our experience has to do with the outward scene of environment, it is still true that we only know anything when the mind inwardly interprets it.

The man we see walking down the street might seem very real, but all we "see" is what the mind interprets as it observes the impulses impinging on the brain through the sense of sight. In fact, it is well-known that two people observing the same outward event will see and report different aspects of it.

We do not need a scientist to tell us the self-evident truth that life, with its incalculable mystery, is the power which has brought us into being. We know that it is the invisible power in the acorn which brings forth the oak tree, or endows a human male and female seed with the ability to become a man or woman.

I emphasise this now because if we are going to experience the greater way of Christ, we must be established in our acceptance of the basic truth that because the Life of God is within us, we have our being in Him, and can therefore commune with Him inwardly. It provides us with a foundation for faith from which all future spiritual progression can leap.

It must, of course, also be true that as God is omnipresent, there can be no "place" where He is absent. His Spirit is like an ocean in which everything is immersed and in which everything arises. Even as the waves on the surface of the sea are each different and individual in their appearance, they are all made of the same ocean and are all identified with each other.

In this sense we can recognise the fact of God everywhere, "outside" ourselves, in every flower or stone, filling the air we breathe, shining in the sun and pulsing in all life and creation. But our most intimate contact must inevitably be always within our own minds and souls, where His Spirit is forever maintaining and awakening our being to greater awareness. That is why the teaching of Jesus, and all spiritually illumined saints and seers down the ages point to this supreme revelation. To be co-heirs and inheritors of the Kingdom of God with Christ is truly the Divine plan and purpose, and must, therefore, be our eternal purpose also. "It is the Father's good pleasure to give you the Kingdom."

So many of these startling statements in the Bible, clothed as they are in poetry and parable, have not yet been generally accepted as a scientific truth which has a profound bearing upon every aspect of man's inherent need for health and happiness, peace and prosperity, and infinite creativeness.

Today we can no longer afford to ignore the inescapable conclusion that, after all, there is an eternal plan and purpose for everyone, and that the way is wide open for the next great awakening. Science and religion rapidly draw together in a common understanding that there is only God, and that we are ready for a realisation of the true facts of spirit and the potential inherent in this recognition.

The Bible makes many references to Light. God said, "Let there be light", and in 1 John 1:5 we are told:

"This then is the message which we have heard of him, and declare unto you, that God is Light, and in him there is no darkness at all."

From the dawn of human consciousness, people who found God in real personal experience have described Him as Light. Consider some of these statements in the Bible:

"Who coverest thyself with light as with a garment" (Ps. 104 : 2).

"While ye have light, believe in the light, that ye may be the children of light" (John 12 : 36).

"For God, who commanded the light to shine out of darkness, hath shined in our hearts, to give the light of the knowledge of the glory of God in the face of Jesus Christ" (2 Cor. 4 : 6).

"Lord, lift thou up the light of thy countenance upon us" (Ps. 4 : 6).

"The people that walked in darkness have seen a great light" (Isa. 9 : 2).

"The Lord shall be unto thee an everlasting light, and thy God thy glory" (Isa. 60 : 19).

"The Lord is my light and my salvation" (Ps. 27 : 1).

"For with thee is the fountain of life: in thy light shall we see light" (Ps. 36 : 9).

These, and many more references, point to the prevailing belief of God as Light. Even the almost lost tribes of Indians in the North American continent described God as "the Great White Spirit".

In more modern times, when we are becoming much more familiar with extra-sensory perception and psychic research and such experience generally, there are countless testimonies of people inwardly, or clairvoyantly, seeing Light so bright that they think of it as the Glory of God.

Then, of course, we have the tremendous conversion of Saul on the road to Damascus. Read it again:

"And it came to pass, that, as I made my journey, and was come nigh unto Damascus about noon, suddenly there shone from heaven a great light round about me.

"And I fell unto the ground, and heard a voice saying unto me, Saul, Saul, why persecutest thou me?

"And I answered, Who art thou, Lord? And he said unto me, I am Jesus of Nazareth, whom thou persecutest.

"And they that were with me saw indeed the light, and were afraid: but they heard not the voice of him that spake to me.

"And I said, What shall I do, Lord? And the Lord said unto me, Arise, and go into Damascus; and there it shall be told thee of all things which are appointed for thee to do.

"And *when I could not see for the glory of that Light,* being led by the hand of them that were with me, I came into Damascus" (Acts 22 : 6–11).

This conversion of Paul the Apostle was one of the vital events in history. Here was a man not even interested in Jesus Christ, except to oppose Him. Yet, unheralded, and on a dusty roadway, he became immersed in a Light which, on his witness, completely transformed him spiritually. Notice, too, that the Light was so intense that he was blind for several days, which only confirms the reality and brightness of the Light itself.

Even more startling, however, is the way his life-work unfolded after this quickening by God. All generations since, in their millions, have had cause to note well the records of Paul's ministry. He became one of the foundations of the Church, and some of the roots of every Christian today draw sustenance from him.

Through this illumination he became the instrument of the Lord. Following such a vision he could not, and would not wish to avoid the responsibility inherent in this revelation. His total surrender released Christ's Light to the whole world in the service given into his keeping.

With the Light comes love, faith, wisdom, understanding, and the Christ power to accomplish all things according to His Will.

How else could Paul have written with such depth and

meaning about Love, as in his letter 1 Corinthians 13. This is of paramount importance to the world today, and so central to the whole theme of prayer and Divine healing that I urge constant and concentrated attention to it, for its importance is profound in every aspect of life and prayer. All who have experienced this baptism of Light recognise it to be Love, and I feel that Paul was trying to interpret the indescribable Light in this way. And this, too, is the teaching of Jesus Himself.

I emphasise these aspects of Light and Love because they represent, for us all, the awakening which is our true inheritance. Everyone, in greater or lesser degree, is already involved in this illumination because Love is Life, and Life is the Light of God. We simply become more illumined as we learn to love more, and follow in the footsteps of the Master with faith and conviction.

* * * *

As a young man I worked five years in Santiago de Chile and Buenos Aires in South America. On returning home I visited one of my school friends who had married. The change in him from our earlier friendship was so startling that I, too, was lifted up to a new realisation by the light that was in him.

He was on fire for Christ. He had had a conversion experience that completely revolutionised his life. We talked until dawn and a new light and understanding awakened in me. I, too, became committed to Christ and, with stumbling steps, tried to follow my Lord. The awakening was, at least, so strong that I saw very clearly that Jesus gave the complete answer to all human needs and problems. I had no difficulty, even then, in realising that Divine healing must be a logical result of love, faith and prayer.

In fact, the Lord fixed this in my mind in a way never to be forgotten. As soon as a bookshop was open next morning I bought a Bible. At home I eagerly unwrapped the parcel, and it fell open at the astonishing Chapter 15 in St. John's

Gospel. As I read it—"I am the true vine, and my father is the husbandman" and all the profound promises and truths which followed, I just knew God was speaking to me personally.

After all the years of experience in a ministry of Divine healing, I can still only witness that I know no more than the promises and truth revealed in those words spoken by Jesus. I only know the Cross of Christ Way, and that it is the Lord Who works. If I seek to offer ever more love, faith, and committal, it is because it is only natural to anyone who really believes and seeks to follow Him.

Shortly after renewing contact with the friend who opened a new window in my soul, I met again another old friend. I had always admired him for his devotion to the Lord and to people, although in the earlier years I was more captivated by the work he was doing for young people in a settlement, teaching amateur dramatics and Shakespeare.

Subsequently he became a Catholic priest, but before this, and shortly after meeting him on my return from South America, he was instrumental in directing my attention to one of the paramount needs in Christian realisation. He taught me the art of Meditation, and gave me a little book to help me along.

How obvious it is when we recognise it! In all simplicity, it becomes very clear that we can only commune with the Lord by abiding in His Presence, making ourselves available to His Ministration.

"Be still . . . and know that I am God" became the main theme of my life and discipline, and down the years awareness of His Presence deepened. It was a repetition of the periods of intense stillness and sense of His Power which I used to get when a boy. Sometimes only the Great Peace. Sometimes clouds of violet light. Sometimes an expansion of consciousness and an intense awareness of infinite Power.

I shall have more to say about meditation later, and only mention it now because it led me into the greatest moment of my life. I saw the Light. Just once! One flash of Perfection! Not long before I was called to this ministry.

One would think, perhaps, that anything really extraordinary in spiritual aspiration would be more likely to be revealed during a quiet time waiting upon the Lord. In my case, it happened when I was not even thinking about God. It came as unheralded Glory.

In fact, I was in a hurry, just finishing a little domestic job standing by the sideboard, ready to go back to the office.

Light! Light! Light! More brilliant than anything I have ever seen or could adequately describe. Brighter than looking straight into the noonday sun. Intense! Unbearable!

It seared through my being in one second-long blaze. It could not have been endured for another moment. Yet, although Light was the power fusing within, it was the Perfection of that Light which was unbearable.

So far as consciousness remained, I was only aware of Perfection stretching to infinity. I seemed to know in that flash the Light of the world, and that all creation was centred in it. This was the Light in all men and it was Perfect Everything, as potential to be experienced for ever.

It was eternal life, love, wisdom and all-knowledge. It contained sinner and saint in its embrace and was the healing of every wound. It was the pattern and purpose in every man, the love of universal grandeur flowing to infallible fulfilment. It was realisation.

Had my body been sick, the sickness would have vanished. Bones would have straightened and cancers would have evaporated.

The perfect Order of God in Whom all life and all worlds rest and have their being.

One moment like this completely changed my way of life. It is the Lord Who doeth the works. Thank You, Father.

No wonder the Gospels, as well as people today, are so inspired to witness to the Glory of God, the Light of the world!

"And, lo, the angel of the Lord came upon them, and the glory of the Lord shone round about them" (Luke 2 : 9).

This writing about illumination reminds me of the inspiration I found in meditation on a mountain peak in California. I would like to share these thoughts with you in the following chapter. But now let us pray.

* * * *

Thank You, Father, for Thou art with us always. In the deep stillness of Thy Presence I worship Thee in spirit and in truth. In the midst of Thy Perfection I am receptive to Perfect Everything, spiritually, mentally, physically and materially, according to Thy Will for my highest good, so I may serve Thee in ever greater ways.

Take my life now, Lord, as I lay it before Thee in love and faith. Reconsecrate me and send me into this day as Thy servant to bear Light to those who may still be in darkness. Help us all to abide in Thy Power and Glory this day and for ever, through Jesus Christ. Amen.

6

By My Spirit

*Not by might, nor by power, but by my spirit, saith the
Lord of Hosts.*

ZECHARIAH 4: 6.

I STOOD ON A MOUNTAIN TOP in California, seven
thousand feet high, and contemplated the vast panorama
of precipitous crags gleaming cream in the sunlight. Redwood forests filled the deep valleys and enfolded the slopes
of a hundred mountains as though raising the bare peaks in
their arms towards the blue heavens.

I was perched, like an eagle, on the edge of a precipice which
plunged a thousand feet to the valley of woodland glades
below. A similar cliff walled the opposite side, and the sun was
already etching a dark shadow across the scarcely visible
cabins of the camp down below.

The air was exhilarating, stirred by the gentlest of breezes
from the Pacific Ocean. I wandered in the warm sunshine
towards the trees away from the peak. The Silence, the
incredible Peace, seemed to enfold my entire being, and
surely God was there. I rested on a grassy slope, and the leafy
branches of the trees framed the mountains and the blue sky.
I drifted from meditation into a Divine sleep. At such
moments one knows that Love is all.

In the dark hours of the night, deep in the valley of the
cabins, I strolled along a path in the forest. A full moon
emphasised the mysterious shadows among the trees, but
surprised the soul with a silver glory spilling through the high
branches. In one glade, I remember, I stepped out of the
darkness right into the clear moon-light and was swept up in

such a vision of beauty and the Father's eternal Presence that this love is inevitably shared with you, now, as you read.

The mountain top, the dark valley; night and day, light and shade, ecstasy and sadness, meeting and parting, birth and death, earth and heaven: all designed by the Great Architect to give us, every one, abundant, eternal life.

Next morning I stepped out of my cabin into the cool wood. Two bears, mother and daughter (or son!) were rummaging in a garbage bin outside the door! They were not afraid of me, and I, surprisingly, was unafraid too! Peace, harmony and love.

Truly we should pause, in awe and worship—every day— before the miracle and mystery of the life which the Father has given us.

When we are not drowned in the commonplace, and our spiritual vision is quickened, we can behold and savour the irresistible variety of experience which flows from the moment we are born until we soar on the wings of spirit on the greatest adventure of all.

We all have our mountain-top experiences and we all, from time to time, walk through the valleys of darkness. We need urgently to know that our eternal unfolding can only proceed through every kind of contrasting circumstance. No power, even the deepest darkness of sin or sickness, can ever break the eternal love which is God's life within us. Always His Spirit undergirds us and eventually leads us to the mountains into the Light again—and somehow we shall have grown in compassion, understanding and faith when salvation comes.

The whole world of God's family is involved in this drama of an eternal life and inevitably must discover its heritage in order to become established in the wondrous ways the Father has prepared for every one of us. And, under the Law of Love so comprehensively revealed by Jesus Christ, we learn to arise as the sons and daughters of God, co-heirs of this immeasurable Kingdom of Life.

Secondary only to the truth that we live, and move, and have our being in God, is the realisation that we are one with each other in His Spirit. We are more than brothers and sisters, for we are part of the unfolding of the one Life of the Father.

That is why we can help one another, and walk more surely together along these eternal highways. If we are uplifted in the real love, and live close to the Lord in faith, we inevitably inspire others to experience the same joy. On the other hand, when we are cast down in the darkness of hatred, bitterness, sin or fear, we also throw a cloud around those whose lives immediately touch ours, and in some degree upon all humanity.

In spiritual work today, perhaps the greatest discovery has been the power of love, faith and prayer in leading friends out of their valleys of darkness and despair up the trail to the sunlit mountain top. Love, Faith, Hope and Prayer are the most infectious, most powerful, and most practical of all human qualities. They represent the highway of the Spirit, and are transcendental in their eternal significance for everyone, everywhere.

The more we become committed to, and familiar with, the realisation that all is Spirit, the more surely shall we consciously be aware of Christ expressing His Power as the Life which is our own being. Within the mountain or man, there is only God.

Throughout history, people have always accepted the obvious truth that God exists. Even in the early days of dawning self-awareness, this instinct was predominant, even though the realisation was focussed on worshipping gods of the wind or weather, sun, or idols of stone. Every religion has always been based on this central understanding, however imperfectly expressed. As man awakened to greater mental capacity, his spiritual consciousness also became clearer, which gave rise to the concepts of Buddha, Mohammed and other prophets or mystics.

Even today, probably two thousand million people give their allegiance to religions other than Christianity. However much they may vary in detail, the fundamentals of all these forms of religion are love, faith and communion with God. It is a salutary spur to tolerance and understanding to realise that had we been born in India or the Middle East, we should have been taught from the cradle to accept and practise the spiritual doctrines of Buddha or Mohammed.

Wedded, as we probably are in the West, to Christ, we must also extend our reach of spiritual understanding to embrace World Brotherhood as an essential commitment of Christ's own teaching and as the most urgent factor in world affairs today. And the best way for us to do this is to seek to be Christ-like ourselves and demonstrate His Love in absolute compassion, tolerance, and understanding of the views of others.

Probably the greatest sin of all is to be self-righteous and lose sight of Love by promoting conflict between peoples of differing religious beliefs. The very essence of Christ's life is the Love that embraces all people in a comprehensive freedom in which judgment or condemnation has no part.

The one need of humanity is to become united in concept and practice as a world family. And Love is the only principle whereby this unity can be established. It must begin, always, with the individual as he arises in this Light of the Spirit to behold and believe in the universal Love of God, comprehensively expressed, in all peoples everywhere.

Jesus Christ Himself, the Son of God sent for world salvation, brought the true Light and revelation by which all conflicts can be reconciled and healed. But if we deviate even one fraction from the basic commitment of Love, the Law of universal obligation, to that extent do we raise a barrier between ourselves and His Spirit.

It is sad indeed to see how much division there has been even between the many denominations of the Christian Church. In days gone by especially, the rivalry and dissension was often so intense that persecution, bloodshed and conflict became often the standard of fanatical Christian behaviour. Today we are at least emerging from this dreadful intolerance, and an ever-increasing degree of unity is being awakened between all Christian churches.

There is still very much to be done in this direction even though some churches have this vision well in mind as a true objective. The difficulty always lies in human frailty. As yet the only partially awakened personality is so quick to judge, so ready to fight for the particular doctrine or belief which he regards to be true. Conflict follows when he thinks someone else is deviating in some way from his own personal conviction, and either arrogantly or passively goes into intolerant opposition.

Perhaps we have not yet fully understood that ultimate truth, that God is infinite and, therefore, unknowable in His fullness. We can only know in part. We can experience God and all His Perfection in a thousand ways, but only according to our need and patterned by the degree of our love, faith and understanding. We are, in other words, involved in a growth, or awakening, which can only come through the processes of frustration and failure, inspiration and achievement, as we experience and assess them.

The sign of the New Christ Age is this understanding that individuals will always congregate together according to their own degree of awakening and follow the vision of truth that is given them. This is the basic reason for the hundreds of differing denominations in the Christian Church. But it is also the reason why we can arise from all spiritual conflict and become united in the one Heavenly Church of Christ. Even as, individually, we live in thousands of different homes in a city, each one moulded to the personality of the family, we are also able to identify ourselves with the community without conflict of interest.

It is the miracle of being that we are all unique, and that we therefore have an infinite variety of interests and ways of expression. It would be impossible even to live at all if we all had to be moulded into identical patterns.

Therefore, even when we believe in the transcendental truth of Jesus, it is inevitable that we shall adopt particular aspects of His Life and Teaching and mould them to meet our own understanding. It will always be a human aspiration to find God by differing sacraments, ceremonial, symbols and forms of worship which fit some inward need and instinct of the individual.

With all this clearly in mind, we can accept and realise the need for the many denominations in the Christian Church, and at the same time accept completely that there need be no inward division at all.

Here is the true secret of unity. Here is the Christ Way into the future. Here is the only way whereby Christians can present a united front of absolute love, faith, integrity and committal to a world that is swamped and in grave danger through disunity.

At this time a very special responsibility is given to all Christians to establish this full truth, because the sickness of the world stems from our failure to implement Christ's teaching on this comprehensive level of love. The Church of Christ, united in Love, aflame with the faith of the early Church, could be God's instrument for solving all the major problems of earth within one generation. In fact, it has, right now, the greatest opportunity to advance this Perfect Awakening than at any time since the days when Jesus came to the Holy Land and redeemed the world through His Cross and Resurrection.

As always, such vision and the fulfilment of it can only come into common practice through the individual. It is no use pointing to the Church in the abstract, since there is no progress in leaving the broad concept floating free, waiting for some intangible "other church" to take it up.

Christianity begins with you and me. It is the life business of each member of a congregation as well as the dedicated committal of a minister. The secret of the early Church was not an exclusive spiritual power revealed by leaders, but the Love of a Living Christ surging into the lives of countless "ordinary" people when they gave their all to Him.

Every church standing today, of whatever denomination,

owes its existence to the truth that family men and women in the early days were so full of Christ that they were prepared to die, as many did, rather than renounce their faith.

We have very little understanding today of the full measure and responsibility of being a Christian. Some day we might well have to face the same kind of sacrifices before the dross which clutters the world consciousness can be purged from it. We have grown complacent and self-satisfied in our material prosperity and, in many areas of our Western world, seldom think the freedom of worship is seriously threatened.

In spite of the appalling pressures and problems inherent in dictatorship and spreading Communism, the Christian, generally speaking, has not yet fully awakened to either the danger or the realisation that a full committal to spiritual principle alone can save the situation.

The early Church in Christ was a spiritual revolution that had to win its way against the absolute opposition of every established church and governmental authority of those days. Christ Himself went to His Cross on the wave of this opposition, and those who followed Him were in daily danger from the accepted powers of the land, spiritual and temporal.

But the people, as they found the transforming power of Jesus, could not be stopped. They were filled with the Holy Spirit, and in God's Strength opposition crumbled away through the demonstration of love, faith, healing, courage and sacrifice, which qualities were the hall-mark of those who followed Christ.

One day I was in Rome. I went into the vast amphitheatre of the Colosseum. On entering this relic of ancient days I was held spellbound as my mind swept back in time to the world-shaking events which took place there.

Much of the great walls still stands intact. The galleries rise, tier upon tier, from the central circular floor of the arena. The floor itself has long since disappeared, leaving only the stone beams through which one can dimly see underground caverns. The pink stonework glowed warmly in the setting sun, and somehow this drew my thoughts mystically into the past and made this place as hallowed to me as an ancient cathedral.

I could so easily imagine the Colosseum in the days when Rome was the capital of the world, and Caesar an emperor before whom millions bowed and served. It was built about fifty years before Christ was born, and when Christianity moved its fire into the heart of the Roman Empire, all the sporting events and displays of pomp and power were staged there. One could so easily think of glittering pageantry, of rich nobles and their ladies, captains of the Roman legions and all who could gain the privilege of entry, filling the galleries as we would fill Westminster Abbey for a Coronation.

On the opposite side of the arena floor is a simple wooden cross. And I remembered that, as the sport of kings and their court, Christians were led in to be torn down by hungry lions released through the gates on the side.

It was their penalty for being Christians, for breaking the laws of the state, which decreed they could not follow Jesus. And they went to their death singing and praising the Lord.

In those days, death was the sentence hanging over the heads of people like you and me who wanted to meet in His Name. With this knowledge, they still met in secret. When they were traced, they died. You will remember, for example, that Christians used to meet in the catacombs of Rome, and that, on discovery, hundreds of them were entombed, leaving only their witness to posterity.

But the acts of the Christians were so potent in the demonstration of this transforming power of Christ that they resulted in pagan Rome and millions of her subjects becoming Christians!

The Church today, then, is founded upon a tremendous love, sacrifice and willingness by simple family men and women of old to give their all to Christ and the truth they knew would save all mankind.

What would we do today if, in changed circumstances, it became a governmental decree that all church services were prohibited, and that the penalty for congregating anywhere in Jesus' Name was death?

Millions are committed already to their churches and to Christ. Millions more only go to church to be christened, married and buried. But, I am quite sure, in such an event as total prohibition by dictators, Communism or otherwise, Christians would again be so filled by the Holy Spirit through renewed conviction and faith, that not only would they willingly die for their beliefs, but the resultant power would simply sweep aside the rule of barbarism.

In fact, this is the Call of Christ to us all now. There is no time to wait for intolerable pressures to come right into our own homes to spur us into action. This effrontery to human liberty and to God is already rampant in many countries, and it is our Christian responsibility and opportunity to become united now and to reveal to a weary world what real love and faith can do.

As of old, it is a personal responsibility. Christ can only work through the individual dedicated life. It is your love and mine which count in the Courts of Heaven. And when more and more people really understand this, and bring this degree of committal into the church, irrespective of denomination, and linked with the concept of Christian Unity, we shall see the Light of the World shining so intensely that all darkness will be swept away.

Nevertheless, in spite of this emphasis on personal dedication and discipline there is another paramount factor which none can afford to ignore, because recognition of it speeds up the entire process of spiritual awakening.

Not by might, nor by power, but by my spirit, saith the Lord.

We need to grasp in a much more personal and intimate way the significance and potential of the fact that God is omniscient, omnipresent, and that we have our being in His Spirit. The vision of the New Age is really based on this knowledge, because we can now scientifically apprehend the truth of it. "Lo, I am with you alway" is no illusion, but a demonstrable fact.

The Father stands there with each of us, holding us in the eternal embrace of His Spirit, and knowing that in His care we shall gradually awaken to a knowledge of His Presence and Power and eternal growth. He knows that free will is His greatest gift to us, and that we can only ascend to fulfil His plans by learning how to use the Christ Power. He knows that when we trespass across the Laws of Perfection we shall hurt ourselves but, like a child learning not to play with fire, we shall progressively arise out of darkness into light.

For many people it is hard work indeed trying to hold fast to spiritual beliefs, and harder still to put them to practical test and practice. The personal way to complete committal is often a struggle of will, intellectual understanding and baffling things in life which do not seem to fit the spiritual pattern held before us.

All personal effort, wheresoever directed, is fraught with possible limitation and pre-conditioned ideas, including racial beliefs. The powerful pull of human experience in any given pattern is often a great obstacle to the free expression of faith. We are, for example, much more certain about the power of a cancer to kill than we are of the invisible presence of God to heal it. We are much more committed to a belief in the money which comes our way as salary, investment or accumulated reserves than we are to a Father Who is the invisible provider of all things, including supply.

Therefore, we can only really break free into the greater consciousness in Christ when we also become completely identified in faith, belief and unlimited conviction that we live in God, and that God lives in us. When we stand aside to allow Him to awaken us, then we can begin to reconstruct our ideas as to what the Presence of God can reveal in every form of experience. To know that the Lord is much more interested in revealing His Spirit to us than we are even able to awaken to it ourselves, is a tremendous incentive to stabilise our lives on this level.

If there is only God, it is a self-crippling limitation to cling so tightly to personal creativeness on our own, when the infinite resources of God yearn for free expression to magnify personal realisation and progression.

With Jesus, we can then stand aside to behold the Glory of the Lord. With Paul, we can walk along our own Damascus road and let the Lord have His Will and way with us.

In this way we arise from self-effort, and pay far more attention to the constant belief that the Father is revealing Perfect Everything, night and day, in the right way and at the right time, for our highest good.

Our personal contribution, as always, is the humble offering of our own very simple, but comprehensive faith; linked with a love which recognises the Lord's Presence, and the complete adherence to the first and second commandments of LOVE.

We accomplish relatively little by might or by power, no matter how strong we may seem. But when we become identified with the Spirit of God then, indeed, all things become possible.

The change from *doing* to *abiding* naturally involves a change of concept. We shift our standpoint from self to God, basing this on a comprehensive acceptance of the truth of His Life in us. Therefore, it is His Spirit which motivates our thinking and our actions. It represents conversion in its highest form of expression and, inevitably, intensifies the entire experience and all its manifestations in church, home, business and personal contacts.

It is an intensely practical experience, since God can only express His Will through man in the midst of the personality and environment. This will touch the man working in a gold mine in Africa or a business tycoon on Wall Street. The little housewife will know His Strength as surely as a politician will be inspired with new vision and power to achieve great goals. The communicant before the altar could become a new Wesley, or the minister quicken the whole church. There is no limit, and no failure on the part of God to fulfil that which is true to our personality and His plan for us.

It remains only for us to fulfil our part by a complete giving of love and faith in His Spirit of Perfection. It is the

Father Who works. We are instruments through which He fulfils His purposes, as we make ourselves available to Him.

It is within this pattern that we can see the true significance of meditation, or being still before God.

Waiting upon the Lord, resting, abiding in Him needs to be electrified with the thrilling awareness that we are actually entering the inward Kingdom of the Most High. It needs the stimulation of absolute belief that NOW, in the stillness, in the midst of God, He moulds, heals, inspires and awakens us to the Perfection of soul, mind, body and circumstance, according to His Will and knowledge of our eternal good.

In the Presence, there is nothing to do apart from realising God. It is the Father Who ministers. We are at the receiving end of Perfect Everything. And, as we practise this soulyearning to be still, one with the Lord, we are led into the Great Silence, into the Peace that is not of this world.

Like the sunshine, it requires no motivation from our side. The Spirit is the life of man, and it is always there awaiting our recognition. When we become still, with that high vision and faith, we are actually partaking of His Perfection, immediately, just as we would instantly partake of the sunshine when we sit in it to sunbathe.

Be still . . . and know that I am God.

One often sees the outward demonstration of this truth in ways even more remarkable than Divine healing, and the following story is a powerful example of this.

* * * *

I was attending a Camp Farthest Out at Ardmore in Oklahoma, and there met again many friends whose lives constantly reflect the full Christ Way.

The Camp was held at Lake Murray Lodge, surrounded by wide acres of parkland and trees, and situated on the edge of a large natural lake. The choice of establishment for these camps is surely one of the central inspirations of this Retreat Movement. It always takes us city dwellers into the peace of the backwoods and this, in itself, opens more easily the door of the Kingdom in which we seek to rest.

The C.F.O. is always a witnessing movement. There is nothing more stimulating than Christian witness to the practical transforming power of the Lord. And 500 people had come from all over the United States and Canada (and England!) to share this time of fellowship and revival in Christ.

But what inspired and strengthened me most was a little crippled lady. Everyone has a natural compassion for those who are handicapped and whose lives are inconceivably limited compared with our own. I saw her first when I walked into the Great Hall. In the midst of this throng of people, she was lying in the centre aisle, at the back, on a stretcher.

Under an impelling compulsion I walked straight to her, and knelt by her side. I have never seen anyone so completely radiant in Christ as she was. Her poor crippled and wasted body ceased even to be important before the love shining in her eager face.

We talked and prayed together. But I felt that she was really ministering unto me. Certain it is that the Christ Power in her led us both into the Presence in the same way a child can do.

For me, and for many, she was a Light of the Lord in that Camp. She was proving to everyone that a physical disability, even when as grave as hers, was no obstacle to the Glory of the Lord. And He certainly used her that week in ways transcending any physical healing, as a living witness of the heights to which a human soul can ascend even through desperate situations.

We felt very humble and strangely inspired by the constancy of this Light of love, courage, faith and committal. I think we marvelled, and perhaps wondered inwardly if our own love and faith would have emerged victorious, should we have been called to pass through such worldly shadows.

By her example, I felt that we were all infinitely stronger

through her weakness. And I somehow think we all shall certainly be more sure of our victory in countless ways, because we saw Christ in a crippled girl.

*   *   *   *

Thank You, Father, *that we are more than conquerors through the redemptive love of Jesus Christ our Lord.*

In thy Spirit, neither death, nor life, nor angels, nor principalities, nor powers, nor things present, nor things to come, nor height, nor depth, nor any other creature, shall ever be able to separate us from Thy love.

We abide in Thy Presence NOW, Lord, and arise filled with Thy Power and Glory, eager to bear witness to Thy love in thought, word and deed in every aspect of our lives, and our own fellowship with those we meet this day and always. Amen.

7

Mother of Mankind

When Jesus therefore saw his mother, and the disciple
standing by whom he loved, he saith unto his mother,
Woman, behold thy son! Then saith he to the disciple,
Behold thy mother!

JOHN 19: 26, 27.

AS THE SPEED of man's intellectual awakening is mounting in intensity day by day it becomes more and more imperative that every spiritual horizon must correspondingly expand to provide a pattern in which to frame it. Intellect without love and wisdom to guide it is as dangerous as the wars it can conceive.

It is impossible fully to understand and appreciate the heights and potentials of spiritual principle without also grasping the significance of the way God brings forth the manifold aspects of creation which we behold in all life and the planet on which we live.

Love, that mysterious dynamic beyond the power of man to analyse or define, is the highest pinnacle of experience. Whenever it floods, like sunshine, into man or woman, it transforms all our thinking, quickens the entire being, and releases ecstasies and creative power transcending every other faculty.

Beginning from the central flame suffusing man and his mate, its power radiates in countless creative ways. It strengthens the mind, quickens the imagination, and harmonises the body. It touches the well-spring of God in the bearing of children and, as long as it shines brightly, fills any home and family with peace, harmony and joy. It brings the same creative power to bear on the arts and crafts of every vocation, with corresponding joy in the fulfilment of work well done.

The entire life-experience is governed, without exception, by the degree of love which is operative. Whether this be expressed in the love between man, woman and family, or in the life-work and relationship with others, the simple and observable truth is that Love is the dominating factor in the mind of man.

No words can ever emphasize sufficiently the paramount importance of this truth. And if we are going to advance safely into the New Age that our mental awakening is thrusting upon us, we cannot afford to ignore the study and cultivation of this force. It is the mainspring of life itself and our highest inheritance as the sons and daughters of God.

For too long we have accepted the gift of Love in a haphazard way. We glow when we have it. We are miserable when we lose it. The race, as a whole, has only followed indefinable instinct in this connection, and has given relatively little thought to cultivating this quality as the *first* essential to a healthy, progressive and happy life.

From the dawn of consciousness we have, of course, always recognised the joy and creative thrust of love between men and women and their children. We have always realised the power of close friendships and the joy of fellowship in worship. But, too often, we circumscribe and limit the Law by seeking to possess the people or things we love, or become dependent upon them, and thus frustrate the greater fulfilment and freedom of total surrender to God.

It is the mystery and paradox of this little known Law that people, work or money (including every facet of needful possession) become fully our own when we learn to release them in freedom or in service for the well-being of all.

The release and the freedom fulfil the Law, and that which belongs to us truly becomes our own. In this way we enter the fullness of Divine Love, which is the principle of absolute and endless giving in creative expression.

With Paul we can truly proclaim that without love, we are nothing. Think back on 1 Corinthians 13, for in it lies the true secret of perfect fulfilment, the secret of prayer and Divine healing—it points the way into the eternity through which we must all travel.

We observe that when love is absent in a home, the flame of life flickers in pain and problem and often sin and sickness. The roots of most troubles in the world are grounded in this tension, which always erupts in human nature when love is lacking. Any psychologist today will point to this inward cause, to the frustrations, worries and tensions, which reflect in manifold ways, discord, disease and dissatisfaction.

When children are divorced from love, they are like young plants shrivelling from lack of water. Indeed, much disease and disaster in adult years spring from the love-starvation endured when they were defenceless children. But, whether a baby or a business man, a queen or a girl in an African kraal, there is neither peace nor well-being unless or until Love comes in to fulfil the high purpose of God.

Our failures represent the degree of limitation we imposed on this Law in its infinite potentials of use. We accept, of course, that the evolution of man can only follow his vision, and that the failures in our personal and world system represent his ignorance of this high spiritual principle. They are the birth-pangs which, in the end, will bring forth the perfect man in the image and likeness of Christ.

But now we are swiftly moving into a new dispensation, and must harness the power of intellect to comprehend all the laws which govern life on earth. At this time, the overwhelming realisation of the power of mind, which has so excited the world society in its ability to master and mould the material of earth in a million new ways, is out of balance with Divine Law.

We concentrate on cultivating the intellect and educate our people to use it, and the accumulated knowledge it can embrace through books, in a variety of specialised ways. We go from strength to strength and, in the proven experience, we really understand that there is a horizon of unlimited possibilities awaiting our exploration.

When I was a boy it was adventure indeed to tickle the crystal of the new wireless set with a "cat's-whisker" and receive music through the air. "Tin Lizzies" were coming as new marvels from the Ford factory, and electric lighting increasingly banished the old gas jets or paraffin lamps.

Today our youth lives in an age of television and jet planes, atomic energy and space ships, and quite expectantly looks forward to the day we can travel to Mars. But we have also suffered from the worst eruption of sheer barbarism the world has ever known.

It began for me when I was a small boy at the dawn of the 1914 war. I saw, for the first time, blood shed in violence when three German warships appeared in the bay around which our peaceful town clustered, and poured a holocaust of explosive into our streets and homes. A shell burst in an alleyway through which hundreds of people were fleeing. My father was pushing a pram with my baby brother, and we two older ones toddled along with mother. And many people died or were maimed.

The zeppelins began to raid our country, and we really thought the world was coming to an end. One night we were huddled in the cellar of our home sheltering from these "little" bombs and shrapnel when a roar of cheering swept across the town. We all stumbled out into the street.

The raiding airship was blazing from end to end. It broke in half and fell into the sea. I remember crying. Somehow the spirit in me cried, I think, for the men who were burning in the sky.

Nowadays, of course, we have grown out of such childish things as zeppelins and primitive bombs. We are so clever that we can kill people by the million, and devastate a city, a country or a civilisation in a day. And everyone on earth, without exception, has been diminished, hurt or crucified, as intellect brushed aside the Law of Love.

Neither man nor nation can break this immutable Law with impunity. The history of disaster, in every form, points with sure finger to this underlying and apparently little known cause. Man or nation losing sight of this spiritual vision loses the way, and arrogantly strides out into a barren wilderness where he could, quite easily, reach the point of no return.

In spite of the power of darkness, often in high places; in spite of the prevailing ignorance of the full import of love, faith and prayer, there are many signs that the law of compensation has set in. The pendulum which swung so wide and high in intellectual aspiration, has now begun to swing back to produce the perfect balance in the awakening of love, wisdom and the full expression of spiritual principles.

However much we may cherish the thought of personal power and self-dependence, the universe still belongs to God, and He has ways and means of teaching us our lessons that we only dimly understand. He needs no instruction from us as to how He achieves the miracle of life or the fulfilment of His creative objectives. We should humbly pause before the fact of being, and think on these things.

Throughout nature we observe the handiwork of God, and increasingly marvel at the multiplying variety of life unfolding. The scientist stands in awe before the "energy content" of the tiny atom which is built into the cellular structure of grass, the fruits of the earth, insects, animals and man.

He observes, without effort, the life principle expressed through the law of masculine and feminine union. It operates, invisibly, through the whole scene from the poppy in a field to man himself. It is a balanced and ordered system poised and expressed within the range of the positive and negative, the masculine and feminine principle.

In another way, we recognise this expression of the motivating power as sex, and know that it predominates throughout nature. But we must come to understand, comprehensively, that the Power itself is LOVE. Then, and only then, shall we really begin to touch the true well-spring of creation and take our real steps towards a full communion with God.

In the human experience, we find this in the relationship of man-woman-child. Our great way into the future is consciously to intensify this in our communion with the Lord, and to become centred in the absolute committal that freedom, giving, sharing and creativeness in the common weal are the essential qualities to be cultivated.

We need now to know that Love cannot, and must not, be confined only to the home-life and friends. It is the greatest power we can ever bring to bear in the practical affairs of personal life, business or vocation. It is the central Law of creation. It is our privilege to use it in the partnership God vests in us, as we awaken to the creative purpose which is also fundamental to our lives.

We have departed so far from this vision of Reality that today it is quite customary to believe that Love is all right in its special family setting, but has no place in the hard world of politics, business or career. In this latter field it is considered to be sentimental, a sign of weakness and, together with religion generally, it is excluded from conscious expression.

We seldom realise that politics and business are "hard" only wherever this quality is absent. Fortunately, however, most of us unconsciously release a good deal of love into these realms. We love our work, and whenever we do so, things go well. When we hate it, we are soured by the drudgery, and often slide down the slippery slope of bitterness and resentment.

We form friendships and team together in pursuing a common goal. The "goodwill" of a business is really the degree of love which has promoted happy relationships with employees and customers through good service.

Some day we shall awaken to the true practical potential, and seek by every means of intellect to cultivate this paramount power. Some day it will take its central place in the home, in school, university, and throughout the social structure. The day will come when we shall assess the worth of politician and businessman by the degree of his love first, and his intellectual brilliance and knowledge second.

So we move into a new age of understanding. In this approach we cannot exclude from our pattern the predominant part women are destined increasingly to take in this present world of man-ruling genius.

Even as man is the chief exponent of intellect, so woman is the greater in Love. She understands heights and depths in this mysterious realm which mere man seldom grasps. Her experience of child-bearing, of mother love, infallibly stamped in her racial memory from the beginning, places her in this exalted position of being much more aware of its power, and of God, than man. But it is the Father Who has made us like this—two essential parts of a perfect whole—for it is obvious that man cannot people the world without woman, any more than woman can do so without man. We have all come into being through this union and, in its eternal unfolding, it must ever provide the true consummation of both natures.

Love always unites, in ever widening ways, from the man and woman to the union of communities and countries. When we see an apparent failure of love between two people, or a total lack of it, or when—for some reason unknown—a man or woman have not yet found their love, then the Law of Compensation must irresistibly bring this consummation into manifestation later in life—here or hereafter. There is always the complete union of two souls somewhere, some time, to make the perfect whole in the Divine Order.

In the meantime, whatever our circumstances, our need is always to enhance the present position with an ever-intensifying degree of love, willingly released in tolerance, understanding, patience and service to those around us.

And, transcending it all, there is the consummation which can only be found in our love for the Lord. Here is the eternal unifying principle. Here we find the Love that IS God, flowing in to give us strength in every weakness, peace in the midst of chaos, and the power to move forward with faith and courage into the infinite ways of good that have already been prepared for us.

Since woman, generally speaking, knows more about love than man, she has a tremendous responsibility and opportunity today to bring her gifts forward on the wings of a greater understanding, faith and prayer. She can so easily commune with God when her vision soars to recognise the truth. She can, and will, prove to be the sublime compensating factor in the solution of personal and world problems today.

Man needs love. He needs it desperately. He cannot live in peace or evolve his true destiny until his intellect is balanced in true harmony with God, and in his recognition of balance introduced through the feminine aspect of the Great Law.

The wise woman today will realise her paramount place in this order. The days of mere subservience to man's needs, or passivity in world events, are over. For countless generations man has ruled and moulded his environment, and woman's place has been an inferior one.

This, of course, is a generalisation, for it is equally true that so much of greatness, whenever revealed through man, stemmed from the love, faith and loyalty of the woman releasing her power in the background. But what she has done instinctively in the past can be intensified without limitation when she can do it consciously and through prayer.

Countless men have already had the experience and tremendous incentive which was born in them when they were in love. The newly married couple tackle work and play with stars in their eyes. Happy the man indeed whose wife beholds him perfect, and undergirds him with faith, inspiration and prayer as he goes into action to fulfil his dreams.

It is the endless and potentially growing ebb and flow in this Kingdom of God, in Love, that the inward greatness of souls finds fulfilment. It can be quickened only as speedily as the individual man and woman can accept, understand and implement the law.

It is a singular fact that, right across the world, women far outnumber men in spiritual activities and church membership. It is remarkable only because it reveals how they are more aware of the inward spiritual need than men. It is no sign of the weaker sex, but reveals the inward and saving strength that resides in our feminine counterparts.

What we urge now is the intense quickening of these inborn faculties by complete dedication and surrender to God. We see woman rising like an angel of Light, when her resources are mustered and released through a greater vision of their significance. We see the woman of the future absolutely poised and centred in God's Love, the vehicle through which the Lord can illumine the lives of men and, therefore, the entire society.

This does not mean that we shall see man sent into the kitchen, while mother directs the affairs of the nation or the factory! Rather do we conceive that woman is the fount from which love, wisdom, faith and guidance can flow. Her inward influence is infinitely more potent than the action in which men are generally involved. She is like a power station. Man will gladly use the power she provides in a thousand ways and, increasingly, will himself learn the arts of love, faith and prayer. Then the perfect whole stands forth, a united channel through which all things become possible.

Increasingly, of course, women are also taking their place in every field of activity and creative work. Their influence already extends far beyond the home when circumstances lead them out into the world in their own right. What government, church, hospital, office or factory could even function at all without their service? How much greater can their service be when they recognise their true potential and proceed to be silent—and sometimes vocal—Ambassadors of Christ unto their communities.

As I travel far and wide, my soul is stirred by the spiritual adventures of faith which women accept and execute. Across the world scene they are working in churches, spiritual organisations, prayer groups and countless other ways, with a conviction perhaps not equalled since the early days of the Christian Church. And I, of all people, have cause to give thanks for the love of family, the women who serve in our Sanctuary, and thousands of others who have contributed so much in services connected with our mission in many countries.

It was a woman who opened the door of our first Sanctuary in this ministry. I had reached the point of total committal and was ready and willing to follow the Christ Who called. My guidance was to open a Sanctuary of Divine Healing in the Name of Jesus Christ, and to go forth without money or conditions into His service.

I inserted a small advertisement in the local paper asking for a room, hall or church to be used for Christ healing through prayer, and received one reply, from a Mrs. Willings. On meeting this benevolent old lady, she said how interested she was in this work and offered me the full use of a large room in what had at one time been her private hotel. The Lord sent it, and I thankfully accepted it.

It transpired that she and her husband had worked this hotel for many years. He died, and she sold it. A month or two prior to my meeting her it became empty, fully furnished, and for sale again. She felt a compulsion to buy it for, she thought, sentimental reasons so that she could freely visit her old happy environment. She had no intention of re-opening it as a hotel.

A few days before my advertisement appeared she was talking with her niece in the long dining-room. They felt a strange stillness, which the niece broke by saying, "Auntie, wouldn't this room make a lovely healing sanctuary?" The Lord had already opened the way, and we certainly learned of His ways in Divine healing there.

One day an elderly lady called, bringing with her a friend who needed healing prayer. Her name was Mrs. Mary Cryer, and she was destined to take a vital place in our unfolding work. Even as we prayed together, I felt God's love radiating through her.

The next time she came, she said on leaving, "If ever you need a new sanctuary, I would like you to know that a wing of my house will always be available."

Shortly afterwards, Mrs. Willings died and the property had to be sold. We simply moved into the lovely new accommodation which He had already provided. Our fellowship in Christ, with "Mother Mary", as we affectionately call her, has grown down all the years. She cradled the new ministry in many ways, and her faith, love and prayer power were—and still are—a constant source of strength, courage and inspiration.

Many years have passed since the growth of our work made it necessary to take over the large buildings where we now have our Sanctuary and offices. But "Mother Mary" still serves in day-long prayer in the stillness before the Lord. She is, as I write, eighty-four years old—full of light, joy, peace and power, and still doing her greatest work.

This reminds me of the many adventures of faith through which our Crusade evolved. Solely as a witness to the Power of the Lord, I thankfully share some of these experiences with you in the next chapter.

* * * *

Help us, Lord, ever to cherish the special gift of Thy Love in the Mothers of Mankind. May they be inspired to reveal the Light of the world by example, teaching and through prayer, and thus be channels of Thy Strength to their children and menfolk.

And we pray that, by Grace, the vision of men may be quickened to realise the full spiritual significance of the man-woman partnership in the eternal unfolding of Thy Will for perfect fulfilment.

Thank You, Father, for their love, loyalty, purity, and selfless dedication to those whom you give into their trust and keeping. Amen.

8

The Sanctuary

*Verily, verily, I say unto you, He that believeth on me,
the works that I do shall he do also; and greater works
than these shall he do; because I go unto my Father.*

JOHN 14: 12.

I HAVE A GRANDSON named Ricky, and a grand-
daughter whose name is Rachel. The boy, as I write, is
nearly two and the girl just over one year old. We have
not seen very much of Rachel yet as her parents lived, until
recently, at Bristol, two hundred miles away. Ricky's home
is only sixty miles from Blackpool, so his visits to our Sanctuary* have been more frequent.

Rachel is a well-built, energetic little angel, at present
engaged in the outstanding adventure of learning to walk
and saying the words she is rapidly accumulating. Ricky is
sturdy and strong. His blue eyes twinkle in a round face
topped with flaxen hair. And, being older than Rachel, he
races about, explores every drawer, hangs on to Sheba's tail,
and is generally just exulting in the joy of living.

Sheba is an Alsatian dog. Three times the size of Ricky and
Rachel, she patiently allows them to use her as a pillow or a
plaything involving everything from leap-frog to bone-
stealing. Of course, Sheba knows she must set the children a
good example of love, tolerance and understanding, because
she is a dog of prayer.

When the bell rings every morning at nine, Sheba goes the
rounds to marshall all the family and the Sanctuary staff, to

*The address of the Sanctuary is 476 Lytham Road, Blackpool, Lancs.

bring them into the Healing Intercession Service. Satisfied that all are present, she gives me a big lick as I sit on the low prayer-stool before the altar, and then flops down beside me in the Silence to pray for all the animals in the world and (I hope) for the cats she has scattered in the past and the cats she hopes, I suspect, to chase in the future!

Whenever Ricky was visiting us, I naturally took him into the Sanctuary with me. No matter what he was doing, nor however excited he was, the moment I sat down before the altar with him on my knee he snuggled into my shoulder, became perfectly still, and usually spent the entire period looking up into my face as I prayed. The expression on his face was so wonderful that tears were not far away.

As he grew a little older, this sense of the sacred nature of prayer became strangely intensified in him. As soon as he could hold the bell we went the rounds with Sheba, gathering in the flock, with Ricky very seriously tinkling the gong. He seemed to know instinctively when it was prayer-time because, just before nine o'clock, I would come looking for him and, invariably, he lifted up his arms to say in baby talk, "Prayers, grand-dad." Very often he is in the midst of having breakfast, but he cannot get out of his chair quickly enough to go into the Sanctuary.

My son, Conrad, who was a psychologist in a mental hospital in Bristol for three and a half years, has now given his life to the Lord, and has come to serve and minister in our World Healing Crusade Sanctuary and offices. So now we have Conrad, his wife Barbara, and the lovely Rachel living nearby.

On the last occasion my daughter Margaret, her husband Dale, and Ricky were visiting us, I had the opportunity of taking both Rachel and Ricky together into the service. And, as we sat before the altar, one on each knee, we knew that we were in the real heaven, and that all our prayers were being answered. We felt that every child in the world was blessed because these two babies were in prayer.

The greatest service, bar none, which any mother or father

can render on this earth is to cradle their children, from the beginning, in prayer, which keeps them open to the love of God. A new generation of people with the Christ-Vision in their eyes would spring into being if everyone, from mother to minister, and all who have to do with the care of children, would bear them up to God in love, faith and prayer.

These words appear in *The Kneeling Christian.*

"Prayer is our highest privilege, our gravest responsibility, and the greatest power God has given into our keeping.

"Prayer, real prayer, is the noblest, the sublimest, the most stupendous act that any creature of God can perform."

The central purpose of our work is to serve others. It has never been our guidance to set up a new chain of churches, or to initiate a new movement with specific membership. We need a sanctuary, a church, in which to pray, but this is only part of the entire organisation which is inevitably necessary to provide the means whereby the wonderful people who work with us can make their service to others effective and possible.

Great service, in any vocation, can—as already described— only be achieved when people unite in a common vision and objective. This is more profoundly true in spiritual work. In this we, and every church, have the opportunity of revealing to the world what real partnership with Christ and with each other can accomplish. At this time in history, whoever is concentrated on emphasising, teaching and practising the spiritual principle, is engaged on the most important work on earth.

We have, therefore, for these many years served, by the Grace of God alone, steadfastly holding this vision before all people He drew into our orbit. We live only to serve and advance the spiritual work and understanding of all other churches, organisations and people. We are not guided nor inspired to seek any kind of self or organisational power. Those who so loyally serve with us have only one supreme objective—to give our *all* to Christ and to mankind without conditions or price of any kind. We do it like this because we believe completely that this is what Jesus would do, and that it is what He wants us to do.

So the Lord takes our work out across the world on the wings of love. Because it is His Love which motivates it, inevitably it multiplies its expression in more and more people. And, thank God, following this vision of serving others, the work draws people, not to us, but back to God and back to their own churches with greater dedication, love and prayer-power.

In the process we have become identified with many other churches, movements, prayer groups and countless individual people all over the world. People really understand now that we seriously mean it when we proclaim our eager dedication unconditionally to help advance their own church or cause. And, I am sure, this is the freedom of the sons and daughters of God.

We yearn to inspire people to give their all to the church of their own choice. We long to see congregations again filled with the Holy Spirit. We serve with a host of ministers and people who are nowadays working to this end, and know we are all one in Christ, engaged equally with everyone else in the One service. When the Lord takes charge, it would be extraordinary indeed if we saw no great works, for that is what He promised.

The most vital factor in our crusade for Christ transcends Divine healing, important though that is. The real power is generated through the consistent and undeviating teaching of Love in service and in prayer, resulting in transformed lives, conversion, and the action of immeasurable good radiating through them into their own churches and environment. The Lord has really harnessed the love and prayer-power of a world-wide chain of intercessors who, in turn, are quickening the spiritual life and aspiration of the whole.

As I survey the Sanctuary scene day by day, I never cease to marvel at God's handiwork. The offices throb with activity; typewriters clack in the various rooms, duplicators whirr, and the electric addressing machine stamps scores of thousands of names and addresses on paper which will travel across the world to bear spiritual information and help to people in need.

It is fascinating to realise that such truth will drop through a letter-box in New York, reach a man in Nigeria, or come in on the mail-boat to a woman in the Pacific island of Tonga. Or change the life of someone half-a-mile away!

Not far away, the printing works churn out an ever-increasing flood of our monthly magazine the *Crusader,* a mass of spiritual booklets, and all the other material essential to office work on this scale. It is so interesting to see the genius of man manifested in printing presses, folding and lino-type machines. And there can be no greater thrill than to see all these men and women engaged day by day producing material which can influence the lives of people anywhere on earth.

It may be a far cry from a printing works in Blackpool to an African village in Ghana, but how much more should we marvel, and give thanks, that today it is possible through the modern inventions of television, radio, printing presses, postal services and speedy travel, to bring the full Gospel to anyone anywhere on earth. There never was so great an opportunity to do this in all the long history of man as there is today.

Every morning hundreds of letters arrive in the postbag, and they come not only from the British Isles, United States, Canada, Africa, Australia and New Zealand, but often from the most unexpected places. It is a stirring experience to meet in the mail a spiritual friend in the Fiji Islands, St. Helena, where Napoleon was imprisoned, or a village in the heart of India or Japan. And sometimes imagination runs riot when we receive a letter from the chief of a tribe whose home is in a central African jungle.

With Christ, there is always a very special sympathy and understanding for under-privileged peoples. Love can only be expressed through compassion and a yearning to serve and help those who are not as advanced as we may be. Interested though we are in bringing healing to any wound, it is infin-

THE SANCTUARY

476 Lytham Road, Blackpool, Lancs., England.

[S. F. Gaunt.

THE TAPE RECORDING SANCTUARY

The Studio is located in the garden behind the Sanctuary.

[S. F. *Gaunt*.

itely more rewarding to inspire more and more friends to unite to serve the masses of people who, as yet, have so little.

I feel a deep sense of guilt and compassion when I think of happy children like Ricky and Rachel, and then remember the hundreds of thousands of little ones who grow up in refugee camps or in famine areas. We wallow in luxuries of our advanced standard of living which, of course, is a good objective for all men, but let us not forget the millions who yearn to emerge from their mud huts, an earth floor, a bed of matting and total possessions amounting to a couple of cooking pots and a cow!

We must be deeply concerned for the material and spiritual well-being of the entire family of God, and we of the West have a tremendous opportunity and responsibility in awakening to a new vision of equality and tolerance in our relations with those who have not yet found this degree of culture.

So I am always thrilled that we send thousands of free books and Sanctuary letters to Africans in countries like Ghana and Nigeria, and to India. Often we see our *Crusader* magazine going out to all the children in an African school, and humbly give thanks that, in some way, the Lord is using us to bring spiritual help into those young lives. And every day a pile of letters comes in from them, revealing their enthusiasm and thirst for prayer and teaching.

At seven o'clock every morning the mail comes in, and the Reading Sanctuary swings into action. It is a sacred time, for every letter is a person, a friend. They write for healing prayer, for information or books, to give thanks for healings, or to re-affirm their fellowship in the world-chain of intercessors who serve.

Round the huge oval reading table will be sitting Conrad, Mac, Gertrude, Eileen and Helen, all busy in the quiet consciousness of God's Presence. The letters are read, sorted and separated for appropriate attention. My wife, ever diligent to serve, spends the morning opening the mail. In another office, staff members like Louie and Elsie will be typing envelopes for replies and in a hundred ways our entire staff spends the day typing, filing, packing literature and tape recordings, making out new stencils for the addressing system, and generally expediting the work in every way. And I will be praying, dictating letters, writing, travelling or taking services, according to what the Lord has initiated.

Everyone receives a reply, and our Sanctuary Letter brings spiritual help to meet each need, linked with the deep intercessions taking place as the letters rest on the altar before God. It is vital to realise that we are really tuned-in to the dedicated prayer-consciousness of a hundred thousand intercessors in a world-chain of prayer which, through the time differences between countries and hemispheres, means night and day intercession for those who seek help through the Sanctuary. No wonder healings and blessings reach the people who write in for prayers!

I am really trying to illustrate, not the magnitude of our work, but the magnificence of Christ's ministration when people unite in a common cause of Love. Not one single aspect of this crusade could even exist were it not for the people in the world who serve with us, and the dedicated lives of each member of the staff who make the organisational side possible. We send, at this time, something like one hundred thousand copies of our free monthly magazine the *Crusader* to most parts of the earth. Not one copy could go out without the men and women who serve in the printing establishment.

The work of each and every one is of equal importance. The girl sticking on stamps, the man in charge of the printing press, the friends in the Tape Recording Sanctuary copying tapes for distribution, or the minister taking a service on a mission thousands of miles away, all are doing the one work for the Lord, and none is more exalted than another. He cannot fulfil His will except through every service, and the smallest operation is equal to the biggest.

From the very beginning, it was the Lord's direction that we should be absolutely dependent upon Him for everything, without exception. I repeat this simply because it is so wonderful to bear witness to the practical expression of God's Love, even to such material things as supply. He was asking for total committal and, by His Grace alone, it became possible to unfold this work in a comprehensive giving, with *no charges for any of our services.*

Down the years, every need has always been met. Certainly, it has flowed through the friends who became united with us in our vision, but this was of their own loving, and not through any petitions of ours. The Father knows His own channels, and simply moves them as needed.

I was a business man most of my life, with a very clear idea about the importance of money. My greatest lesson was to "unlearn" all this, to become stripped of all material possessions, and then to be launched out on an "impossible" venture of faith following a concept of Love, with the Lord in charge of an exchequer that did not outwardly exist.

As the work grew, so did expenses, which God handled far more efficiently than ever I could. Never any surplus—only the ebb and flow of expenditure and love-offerings exactly meeting each need. It was, and is, like a river bearing constant water to a city as it flows through it.

It is wonderful to witness to the Lord! One night I awakened and was aware of the wondrous Presence. And knew, in a strange but authentic inward way, that the Lord wanted me to publish a free monthly magazine to send spiritual truth to whoever cared to ask for it. I knew it had to go out without any price or condition.

Within a fortnight the first issue was printed, and sent out to a thousand friends we had come to know through previous service and correspondence. It did not take much business acumen to realise the potentially fantastic costs of printing and postage involved in the multiplying circulation of a free magazine! We had no money, but when the bill came in from the printers it was there to meet it!

Down the years we have sent out millions of copies to anyone and everyone who asked for it. And, with ever mounting and astonishing costs of staff, organisation, printing and postage, the Lord has never failed to pay His way. Never any extra, but always sufficient to meet every need as it arose.

Sometimes intelligent business visitors would suggest going through our scores of thousands of index cards to "weed out" people who never sent offerings! What a travesty and denial of Divine Love this would have been! We have never, ever, knowingly cancelled an address ever since we began except by request, death, or if the magazine was returned as "gone away".

Quite often we are reminded of God's wisdom in this connection, when perhaps we receive a letter from a man telling us that he has been receiving the *Crusader* for years and never opened one issue. Then he was seriously ill, or in grievous trouble, when the next issue dropped through his letter box. Following some impulse he opened it, and found a complete answer to his need and was writing to give thanks.

Our job, yours and mine, if we seek to follow the wondrous way of Christ, is to go all the way with a living faith intent on giving, and giving, and giving until our souls are singing in the love of the Lord. And Love is unconditional in expression.

In England we have what we all call "Fish and Chip shops". Here they fry fish and chipped potatoes, and people can buy them, hot and fresh from the pan, to take home for supper. One evening a lady who was troubled with arthritis went to such a shop. Returning home she found among the outside wrapping paper a couple of greasy pages of our *Crusader* magazine which she idly read.

And, while reading with quickening attention the article about prayer and Divine healing, her pains disappeared and her joints became loosened. Quite some time later she told me this story after a service in her town. She had simply followed the healing by writing in to be put on our mailing list and had never been troubled any more with the arthritis.

The Father never makes a mistake. It was not chance that brought spiritual truth to meet her needs, but the action of God directing the love He desired to release to her at the right moment. That it came in a wrapping of greasy fish and chips was of little consequence when a life was at stake.

*   *   *   *

A vast ministry has also unfolded round our Tape Recording Sanctuary. We have always believed that the modern Church must boldly accept and use every facility provided by science to carry the truth to the people. If business enterprise is based on such efficiency, how much more eager we should be to be efficient stewards and executives in God's Business.

Printing and addressing machines, mechanical office equipment, cars and planes, telephones and radio, postal services and tape recorders, all save time and energy and make it possible to embrace infinite horizons of service.

The power of the written word has been proven so completely that it is, of course, one of the essential factors in spiritual evolution, from the Bible to all the books, magazines and pamphlets which reach far and wide to win souls for Christ.

We have also known for generations the power of the spoken word in His Service. In fact, from the dawn of history, men have proclaimed spiritual truth to the people, and every church is a witness to this fact.

Nowadays, the same word extends right across the world through the media of radio and television. There is no limit to what can be developed in this way, and it will certainly play an ever-increasing part in the spiritual awakening now coming into focus. The Church now has a congregation far beyond the walls of any sanctuary.

Not long after *Crusader* was born, I saw the possibilities inherent in the new tape-recording machines that were increasingly coming on to the market. And so, in very humble beginnings with first one, and then two recorders, a worldwide ministry has grown enabling us to send out an ever expanding output of tape-recorded talks and healing prayer.

Around this time two very good friends, Mr. and Mrs.

Wilson, came into our Sanctuary, and we all began experimenting in this mysterious realm of electronics and microphones. And we produced tapes for distribution, copying them laboriously one by one on the extra machine!

When anyone is involved with new processes of creating something, there is always an attendant joy, interest and excitement. We played for endless hours, usually late into the night, testing, trying, working it all out step by step. The early machines were not so good at that time and we had breakdowns, the wrong pitch of voice, aeroplanes flying overhead to spoil a recording with their noisy engines. A telephone would ring, or someone come bounding into the room at a critical point and kindly offer us a cup of coffee!

But we knew something important was being born, and persevered until the quality we wanted became a reality. Then they began to go out to people who owned recorders, and soon reports came back of healings or blessings which followed the playing of these tapes to people in need, or to prayer groups.

We discovered, in this tape-recording work, that a *state of consciousness* is recorded as well as the words. As we went into the Silence before making every recording, the prayer-power and love released was equally fixed in the recording itself. This proved that whoever subsequently listened to these words also experienced the love, faith and dedication in which they were produced. It is a vital fact which anyone can prove, and is startling in its significance in extending such ministries in world-wide circulation.

Soon we needed more machines and the room began to look "professional" with all its mechanism, knobs, switches and trailing wires. Eventually we had recorders of all shapes and sizes almost crowding us out. And, as demands steadily mounted, we had increasing difficulty in making copies to meet the need.

Somewhere in the midst of this development I had a wonderful experience. Now tape recorders are expensive, and each tape, containing as it does a whole hour of recorded talks and prayer (half an hour on each track) is also costly to produce. So an expanding work in this direction, like printing, is a heavy item indeed from a worldly point of view.

One day I had just begun to write an article about these recordings and what good work they could do for the Lord. Then suddenly I was "caught up" in the Great Silence and, as clearly as any audible word the still, small Voice told me to send all tape recordings out absolutely free of charge to anyone, without exception, who wrote in or asked for one. And with it came a glorious feeling of joy and freedom.

From that moment, thousands of these recordings have gone across the world to all kinds of churches, prayer groups and individuals. It is thrilling to realise that such a work can penetrate into jungle or city, anywhere on earth, witnessing to the cause of Christ.

And, of course, this recording ministry grew accordingly. It is interesting to note, in passing, how love, when unconditionally released, inevitably magnifies its products in countless ways and forms. None of the written or recorded works published by us (with the exception of books issued by other Publishers) is copyright. What we do is given in love and is free for everyone to use.

We soon found that, for example, one of our recordings would be received by a friend in New York. He would invite a dozen people to listen to it. Many of them, possessing recorders themselves, would later bring their machines and make a copy of it. So unknown thousands of extra tapes have gone into multiplying circulation.

I believe, in writing all this about our Sanctuary, the Lord will use these words to help other churches and groups to expand their ministries in the same way. There is such an infinite horizon open for spiritual work that one can only urge every church to go far beyond the boundaries of the walls of the church itself. People in the community and far away can be touched by the Lord when we open the way.

The pressure of work in tape recording became so great that we had to create a special studio down the garden. We removed all our mass equipment into this carefully planned building, we talked and schemed, but were always limited by the time it takes to copy two tracks of a recording taking an hour's talk.

One day I was sitting in the Recording Sanctuary alone, in meditation. This problem came into my mind and my attention was drawn not to the machines, but to the reels of tape. Now I do not know anything about electronics, apart from the general experience of recording and operating these machines. But at this moment I seemed to be given the knowledge that the words spoken were imprinted *electronically* on the tape and that, therefore, it would be possible to copy *both* tracks simultaneously, even though one track would be playing in reverse.

This was vision indeed! I talked it over with Hubert Wilson and we both agreed it could be so. I went to a very clever local electronics engineer, and he immediately saw the possibilities, examined our machines and agreed that adjustments could be made by adding additional recording heads and amplifiers to reproduce two tracks in one operation.

In the end, he standardised all our equipment and built it into professional panels filling the whole side of the large room. To us, then, on entering, it was like coming into an electronic engineer's dream of a recording studio. From any given master tape we were now able to make ten complete copies of an hour-long recording every fifteen minutes. Now we could mass-produce to meet every demand, and all is very well indeed. And the tape recording department is a joy to our friends the Wilsons, the despatching department and to me, as we see our products going out to bless so many people.

Mr. Hamblin used to have a saying, "When the Lord guides, the Lord provides". But He not only provides the funds necessary for so big an enterprise as giving away free tape recordings, but provides the knowledge whereby they can be efficiently made. It is joy indeed to know that anyone, anywhere, can ask for such a service, and for us all at the Sanctuary to feel it is our humble privilege to be a channel

through which can flow the spoken word of Love, in the name
of Jesus Christ.

*   *   *   *

All achievement is measured by the degree in which people
are able to find fellowship one with the other. Beginning right
in the heart of family life, this principle extends through the
entire range of human activity. Behind all the seething works
of the world, and in spite of many injustices and failures, the
central fact remains that there is a compulsive law which
draws people together in service.

This is so powerful that every person on earth is conditioned and motivated by it. No matter what our vocation
or aspiration, we are, from the primitive tribe in a mountain
fastness to the most advanced nation on earth, dependent
upon one another. Whatever we achieve, it is and must be
done in and through relationship with others. No man is
sufficient unto himself alone.

In this we see so much of the undergirding love and wisdom
of God, for it reveals something of the far-reaching purposes in
life. And, to the awakening spirit, it provides a glimpse of the
Divine objective in the Father's plans for His world family.

It is well to pause and consider the significance of these
inward compulsions, because they are more often than not
lost to our vision in the commonplace task of the business of
living. We inevitably follow the pattern, in however limited
a way, but seldom see the greater significance of the inner
truth that leads us towards the high spiritual fulfilment which
is the central purpose of this motivating principle.

The Law which governs all creation is Love, for God is
Love. The first quality of Love is creativeness, both in the
Spirit of God and in man. Its expression, therefore, springs
from the Father and, so far as the individual is concerned,
becomes a "miniature" stream of power leading him into
expanding creativeness.

Since the same fundamental Love radiates through all
people, expressed as life, it is inevitable that the general

creativeness must multiply, for the Law of Love is an eternally creative and multiplying principle. In this it is the Law of evolution or progression.

The other central factor in Love, as Law, is that it operates through giving of its own "being" into the works it becomes interested in creating. The Father, for example, pours the whole of creation into expression through His Spirit. It is, in this context, beyond our understanding, but intuitively we know and experience the full and unconditional "giving" of God in every phase of creation, and in our own lives.

We truly share, and this is our highest privilege, in the creative purposes of the Lord. The world is given to us as part of His Kingdom, and through the gift of life, He gives us the freedom to learn how to share with Him the great Law of Love in the creation of society and its infinite variety of expression.

But, circumscribing a wide range of free will, the compulsive Law forever operates and guides us towards an ever-awakening awareness of its irrevocable nature. This ensures that, consciously or unconsciously, we shall always work, create and serve together, from the family unit and through every enterprise, in mutual inter-dependence and, ultimately, in a comprehensive knowledge of our dependence upon God for His Love, in everything.

We can clearly behold this Law already in operation, whether we have consciously recognised it or not. Although in the outward scene the vision may be lost in our concentration on "making a living", building businesses, wrestling with each other for power or position, the fact still remains that we are, in a thousand degrees of effectiveness, serving one another and giving our lives to it.

The farmer makes possible the food on our tables, and the king in his castle depends on the services of people from coalminers to councillors. The factory produces goods for people, and people team together to make them. The owner of a business owns nothing. He is but a partner with Life and with other people who serve in some enterprise, using the basic products which God has provided and loans to us during the period we dwell here.

No aspect of society can function without the aid and fellowship of other people, and all service, however expressed, flows ever outward to sustain or meet the needs of others. The entire world exists and awakens within this pattern and framework.

Therefore, in the highest sense of truth, all people are not only equal in God's sight, but they are equal in one another. The girl in an office is as important and as necessary as the executive, even as the man who sweeps the streets of a city is doing as vital a job as the prime minister or president who drives along them.

At this stage of our evolution these true values are out of perspective. While the basic factor of mutual inter-dependence always operates, we are still imprisoned by the concept of personal power, property and possessions. We are still governed by a world-wide belief in wealth and assume false authority and position according to our possession of it. If we gain power through the gifts of intellect and knowledge, we often disregard the needs and hopes of under-privileged people, and forget that our position would be empty were it not for the fabric of service emanating in comprehensive ways through every soul on earth.

The New Age of man's understanding will embrace and rectify all these weaknesses in human nature and the social structure. The Law is immutable, and in the eternal reaches of Divine plans, we shall gradually conform to the Law of Love, because therein lies our true fulfilment and progression.

That is why the teaching and practice of paramount spiritual principle has become so important today. We have reached the stage of evolution when we can make no more real progress without bringing it into all our personal, national and international relationships. It is so vital now that the safety and continued existence of the entire race depend upon it.

But the horizon is bright with the dawning Light. The very awakening of intellect causes more and more people to recognise the truth. And, as surely as the sun will continue to illumine the earth, as surely as the Father will continue to maintain it, so shall we all learn consciously to adopt every aspect of spiritual truth as the First Science of life and its greater expression.

It causes us to reiterate the fact that the Church of today has its predestined opportunity and mission to lead the way more boldly than ever before. It is the highway along which all humanity must travel, and it is already built. It is time to throw the gates wide open and organise to direct and handle the traffic which will inevitably flow through them.

All our Sanctuary work has developed round these principles. The people who serve with us have been sent by the Father. They came because they were ready for this new pattern in their lives. And, in this supreme equality before God in His service, the Law is fulfilled. The Lord knows the beginning and the end for us all.

My son, Conrad, has always had a sense of spiritual mission, born entirely in his own consciousness. I believe, so completely, in everyone—and children in particular—evolving the patterns that are true to them, that I have never tried to influence his choice of career. He wanted to be a psychologist and eventually graduated from the university.

It was around this time that he began to feel he would like to serve the Father in our crusade work. But we all agreed it would be wise to go into the world first, and he was given a post as the only psychologist in a mental hospital. Inevitably, with his spiritual vision, he had a deep experience there, both in clinical work and research, and in prayer group activity.

After three and a half years we knew the time had come for this young and eager man to join us. "Behold, I make all things new!" And, indeed, the vision of our expanding service and spiritual ventures with the Lord is quickening us all.

The point I am really making, however, is that the Father plans all things. We merely stand aside and see the perfect patterns falling into position in the right way and at the right time. It becomes effortless when we offer no resistance and allow the Lord to do what He will.

I remember in the very early days how the Father brought the beloved Gertrude into service with us. She had begun to come to a weekly service we used to hold at the Sanctuary when it was in a wing of Mother Mary's home at St. Annes-on-Sea. I always saw the Light in her. Then, one day, in the Stillness, the Lord told me to go to her home and ask if she would like to work in the Sanctuary.

It turned out that her life was so centred in Christ that she longed only for opportunity to serve. Within a week she was with us, and it was one of the most important events which ever took place in our work. She has been a Light indeed to hundreds of thousands of people as she worked in prayer each day. So eager, so dedicated that she, together with "Mac", is at the Sanctuary every morning at seven o'clock to meet the mail, and we almost have to chase them away at night!

Mrs. Mactaggart, our "Mac", is my personal secretary and the poet of the Sanctuary. It would be quite impossible to evaluate the service she has rendered to the Lord, and to me, all these years. And, after all, there is no love greater than the life which is laid down to God and to friends in service.

I met her first in London in the early days, when she came to a service at the Caxton Hall almost blind with cataracts. When everyone else had been ministered to in prayer, she came to me and in the Light of the Lord her eyes became clear and they have been perfect ever since that instantaneous healing. Whenever anything troubles her, we simply pray together, and it vanishes.

Shortly after Gertrude came, I was inspired to ask "Mac" if she would like to join us. And, thanks be to the Father, she did and has been with us ever since, a Light to us all.

It is certainly true in all our crusade work that we could not achieve anything at all if we were not undergirded by such devotion so fully expressed in the sacrifice and service of my wife, Mac, Gertrude, the Wilsons and, indeed, every member of the team of workers at the printing establishment and Sanctuary.

But it is the Father Who works, and it is He Who draws us together whether here in our small segment, in any church or, for that matter, in any and every kind of service or vocation.

Above, below, and behind it all is the Spirit in Whom we all live and move and have our being. In Him we are eternal in nature, and are moving irresistibly forward to fulfil the purposes which He has initiated and implanted from the beginning.

I tell you these few fragments of our Sanctuary history only as a witness to the Glory of God. I pray only that these experiences may hearten and encourage you in whatever way you follow.

And, if we can offer you the hand of love and fellowship in any present need, please do not hesitate to ask for it. Our healing prayers, the Sanctuary letter of help, healing, friendship and teaching is yours to command, week by week. Our free monthly magazine and tape recordings are yours for the asking. Whoever you are, wherever you may be, in Christ, we seek only to serve you, listen to your problems, help you with them, unconditionally, free of charge, expecting nothing but your fellowship as we try together to ascend to greater heights of Love.

In Love, the Law is fulfilled by us, by you, whenever we have the privilege and opportunity to serve.

Thank you, Father. It is so.

*　　　*　　　*　　　*

Upon Thy Table at the dawn of day
With reverent love and tenderness I lay
A tale of grief and human misery,
Sad record of a soul's Gethsemane.
One whose bruised feet a painful pathway trod,
Took up a piteous pen and wrote to God.
His broken life I bring that Thou may'st mend,
This is no letter, Lord . . . THIS IS MY FRIEND.

Bless Thou my comrade, Father! Bless me too!
Re-consecrate our works to Thee anew.
He stumbles, maimed and helpless, to Thy side
Make me his intercessor and his guide.
Speak with my lips and grant that he may hear
Comfort to heal his wounds and banish fear.
Give me Thy Power, Thy ministry Divine,
Oh! may he sense Thy gentle touch in mine.

Within this tranquil room of Answered Prayer,
I lift to Thee the burden of his care.
Bestow Thy priceless boon and let me be
To his bewildered heart Thy deputy.
Wipe out the past and every fruitless vow,
Teach him to dwell in Thy Eternal NOW.
Use me to consummate his glad release,
And through my dedication grant him Peace.
                                        "Mac"

9

Divine Thinking

Finally, brethren, whatsoever things are true, whatsoever things are honest, whatsoever things are just, whatsoever things are pure, whatsoever things are lovely, whatsoever things are of good report; if there be any virtue, and if there be any praise, think on these things.

PHILIPPIANS 4 : 8.

I HAVE LIVED by the sea most of my days and, in some mysterious way, can come very close to spiritual realisation on a beach or in a boat. Some people find this to be true when they are near trees or in the mountains, or even in a garden. I think, in varying degrees of intensity, we are all drawn into a greater awareness of God when we observe the grandeur of nature.

On the western seaboard of Britain the sun sets on the Atlantic horizon, and this coast is noted for the magnificence and variety of the sky-filling glory as it goes down. In the tropics, the sun disappears into the night with startling speed; in England, we have a long twilight before total darkness, and time to appreciate the spectacular display as the last light of the sun sets fire to the clouds and sea.

I have never met anyone who was not deeply moved by this inspiring scene. In the summertime, when hundreds of thousands of holiday-makers come to Blackpool, they throng the miles of promenade edging the beach to watch God turning His world round, as He bids us "Goodnight" in a halo of gold, red, yellow and orange light.

There is something about the clear wide horizon, the depths

of the sky and perhaps the invisible magnetic currents on the coast which bring a deep peace to my soul. I know that many apparently insuperable problems have been solved as I communed with the Lord on these beaches.

When our minds are cluttered with the debris of a lot of negative thinking, and our thoughts swirl in concentrated worry about some grave problem, our real need is always to find God and a corresponding release from the crucifying mental problems which seem to imprison us. We can often find great help in this by making the effort to come close to nature again, and thus enter more realistically into the inheritance of the world which the Father has created for our joy.

If we cannot readily come out into the clean air and behold Him in the panorama of nature, then we can always find Him inwardly in the spirit. And, in any event, we can always look out far beyond the confines of our own world into the sky, even if only through a window.

Whenever I have a pressing problem, I like to walk on the beaches and talk to God about it. The nature of a problem can sometimes be so intense that it dominates our thinking and can, as many people know, bring such tension through attendant worry that even greater troubles or sickness ensue.

Sometimes, burdened with this kind of situation, I have felt my mental attitude change even as I walked across the high tide line and strode out over the sands towards the sea. It has been like the opening of a valve releasing some pent-up pressure, giving a sense of peace again.

Out near the water, as I walk, words of adoration, praise and thankfulness have spontaneously poured from my lips. With my whole being lifted in prayer, in vocal recognition of His presence, an inward assurance has always come that the difficulty was being solved and all was well. It is startling how many real problems have been dispersed on these beaches, and quite often the solutions have already been outwardly manifested, when I returned to the

E

Sanctuary. Others moved through necessary phases of adjustment and were changed in the right way and at the right time.

Out near the water-line I would declare my reverence, worship and love for our Lord, and give the trouble over to Him. Aloud, in a voice full of conviction, I would say words like these:

*   *   *   *

"Thank You, Father, for Thy wondrous Presence. In the Name of our Lord and Saviour Jesus Christ, I worship You and Love You, Love You, LOVE YOU, Lord, with the whole of my being. Take me, right now, in complete surrender, and mould me according to Your Will for more perfect service for others.

"In Your Holy Spirit, Father, I bring before You in love and prayer every soul on earth, all who are particularly troubled or ill in mind or body, and all who seek help through every church and our sanctuary, and I give thanks, here and now, that every one of them is receiving this Blessing.

"I give to You all my mistakes, weaknesses, sins and fears, repenting all these frailties, and know You have taken them all. In Jesus' Name, I thankfully and completely accept comprehensive forgiveness, here and now, and begin again, a new creature in Christ to serve.

"With simple trust I give my present problem into Your keeping, and just know that Divine Perfection fills the whole of my life. I am glowing with Your Love, pulsing with Your energy, radiant with every heavenly joy. Your Spirit is the only reality and I am now correspondingly poised in the Peace and Power of Perfect Everything.

"I accept completely that infinite Good now flows through the entire range of my life to meet every inward and outward need in the right way, at the right time, through the

*right channels, as directed solely by You, Lord, according
to Your Will for me and for those for whom I pray.*

*"Take my life, Father, and melt it, mould it, fill it and
use it in Love to advance the well-being of everyone whom
You bring into my orbit. And now—Thank You, Father,
that it is being done, through the Love, Redemption, Atonement and Resurrecting Cross of Jesus Christ, our Lord.
Amen."*

In the end the positive and powerful words of prayer and
affirmation, spoken aloud, would cease and would be replaced
by a Peace beyond understanding. One only knew that God
was All—here—now—in me, in you and in all, filling the
sky and wide ocean. His Spirit was in every grain of sand
under my feet, and the air was pulsing with His energy.
And, in this simple way, all my thinking was changed for me
in His response.

Prayer is really answered when we come close enough to
God for Him to change the harmful patterns of our thoughts
and mental attitudes. Faith means the acceptance of a new
pattern, which we accept to be completely real. We believe in
the Perfection Pattern, instead of the imperfect one which
was imprisoning the problem.

We have to learn to think and pray in our hearts, that is,
with a conviction which completely dominates both the
conscious and unconscious aspects of our mind. "As thou
thinkest *in thy heart* so wilt thou be".

"Verily, verily I say unto thee, except a man be born again,
he cannot see the Kingdom of God." We have, in fact, to die
to all the old ways of thought and be born, or awakened,
to our identity with the Christ Mind. Then, "The old things
are passed away, behold I make all things new."

When confronted by difficulties, we either want to get them
solved or try to run away from them. When they are intense
enough, they often stimulate us to prayer, and this becomes
effective according to the degree we are able to surrender our
lives, and the problem, to the Father. It has been said that

"Man's dilemma is God's opportunity", and it is a fact that in great extremity wonderful events often follow prayer, for a very good reason.

People are often completely overwhelmed by some burden. They have tried every expedient and skill which they and others could offer, and all have failed. Even those who have perhaps only a slight belief in the power of prayer may well now turn desperately to the Lord as the only possible last resort. This results in giving the entire situation to Him with such single-minded intensity of purpose that the Lord can release the necessary Divine adjustment.

Such a person is often "reborn", for the surrender of everything to God opens the channels of the soul and system to His perfection. Thoughts and patterns are changed by the influx of His Love, and a new way of life emerges.

Every prayer is answered in some way, however feeble our expression of it. The full response may not be visible for a long time, conditioned as it is by the degree of our awakening to love and faith, but it is the beginning, always, of greater experience.

Superficial prayer, although sincere in its expression, may only be words without the intense feeling, faith and committal so necessary. The conscious mind needs to plant its conviction, like roots, in the unconscious mind to ensure a total acceptance of the spiritual truth. We can only think this Perfection Principle "in our hearts" when we are so sure of its all-pervading Reality that it becomes the paramount pattern of our conviction and aspiration. As we are told, "the effectual, fervent prayer of a righteous man availeth much".

Actually, we are all governed to an extraordinary degree by the compulsions constantly emanating from the unconscious, or subconscious mind. Here is the receptacle of every thought we have ever expressed since birth. In the memory lie all the patterns of previous thinking and many racial and hereditary influences. The subconscious collects them all and the patterns resident therein will manifest good or ill according to their quality.

To be reborn, to awaken fully to the Christ Way, means the sublimation of the whole man, which of course also changes the patterns of the unconscious mind and thus releases the corresponding Good. We really reach God through this complete faith in the indwelling Presence and the "imprisoned splendour" then radiates through our entire being.

"The Kingdom of God is within you," said Jesus. It is this kingdom we are asked to seek first, so that we may become identified with this stream of "Goodness" as our natural way of life, co-heirs with Christ.

So, in the daily round, we are all conditioned by the quality of our thinking and it takes little imagination to realise that good thoughts produce good results and evil thinking brings trouble in its train. We live in a threefold dimension of mind —the conscious, the sub-conscious and the Divine—and it is our life-purpose to become attuned to the infinite Perfection, and thus allow it to be released into our outward experience.

In these days we concentrate on cultivating the power of the conscious mind, and generally ignore the significance of transcending sub-conscious compulsions and patterns. The education system crams our minds with knowledge and develops the power of thought to a very high degree. We send millions of young people into the world intellectually awakened, but spiritually crippled, because we do not seriously seek to understand the far-reaching power inherent in the inward nature and our identity with the Father.

We are all very much alive to the power of positive thinking. Courses of all kinds are available to train the memory, induce self-confidence, and cultivate will-power. But few of them recognise the significance of love as a basic principle, or the power of Divine imagination. Prayer, of course, is not usually even considered to be within the scope of such training.

And so, in this vital realm of the mind, we tend to cultivate powers which are out of balance and, therefore, inadequate to fulfil the needs of the whole man. We become involved in mental gymnastics and try, by discipline and practice, to force the mind to conform to mentally induced patterns. No wonder mind training is difficult!

We try to discipline or overcome our weaknesses, and they grow stronger or erupt in new forms of pressure. We try by will-power to achieve what we want and often break ourselves in the process. We become intent on victory by overcoming through the force of our own mental strength, and forget a cardinal principle of mind, that victory is best achieved by love, imagination and prayer, not by will-power.

We endeavour to force or fight our way through every obstacle of personality or experience, and forget another basic principle of mind inherent in what the psychologist would call "the Law of Reversed Effort". This simply means that the more we strain by will to overcome anything, the more power we give to it, with a consequent rebound of a bigger obstacle or weakness.

We can see so clearly nowadays the imperative meaning behind the instruction to keep our minds stayed upon God, upon the Perfect, at all times. That upon which the mind dwells becomes stronger, whether it be a bad habit, worry, resentment, jealousy, lack of money, or any problem or obstacle disturbing us. Likewise, when all thought, in love, imagination and faith dwells upon God, and the Divine Action in every situation, that too is magnified in expression.

The way we create day by day is irrevocably governed by the attitude of mind in the thoughts and actions we initiate, and in our reactions to the thoughts and events of the environment. How vital it has become that we uncover the hidden secrets of life, the mind, and the means to use this paramount gift!

Those who are ready and willing to face this truth will immediately ask, "But how can it be done? It sounds so complicated." And we agree that in the *human* consciousness it is the most difficult of all aspects of life to control. Anyone who has seriously tried will tell of the incredible difficulties inherent in the control and cultivation of positive mental processes. It is one long story of success and inexplicable failures, of endless struggles against weaknesses which, when brought under the pressure of the will, simply project their pressures in the sub-conscious, to erupt later in some other way.

That is why the Lord, in His loving wisdom, gave us the simple secret, which is equally available to the most intellectual professor or to a little widow living in an isolated cottage in a wood, who knows nothing of mental gymnastics.

In Christ it is all done for us, as we collaborate with Him! This is so infallible that it is astonishing we have not clearly understood it already, and introduced it as the central theme of all education and achievement.

Consider the range of thought sequences which destroy positive thinking. Most of them represent, in some way, our departure from the principles of love or faith in God. Hatred (for people, work, or anything else), resentment, bitterness, anger, frustration, sin, selfishness, greed, intolerance and judgment of others, all, in countless ways and degrees, produce the negative thinking and negative action represented by discords, disaster and much disease of mind or body. These thoughts and emotions, in varying degrees of intensity, represent the negative aspect of Love.

Every form of worry, fear, lack of confidence, grief and the dangerous tensions they generate in our relations with people and circumstances are largely born through our sense of insecurity, when confronted by life or problems which we feel inadequate to solve. They demonstrate the degrees of limitation in our faith.

The two factors of the Laws of Love and Faith are central in importance to the comprehensive well-being of the whole man, woman or child. And Jesus gives us the simple answer by revealing the Great Law. He tells us, decisively, that this is the Commandment of universal obligation:

"Thou shalt love the Lord thy God with all thy heart, and with all thy soul, and with all thy strength, and with all thy mind.

"And thou shalt love thy neighbour as thyself."

Never, in all the long travail of man on this earth, has so vital a truth been revealed with such emphasis, in so few words, offering so great results for human well-being.

From a downright practical point of view, if the hatreds, angers and selfishnesses can wreck lives and nations, does it not become important to emphasise and cultivate the opposite positive qualities?

Notice how the transformation of our thinking takes place. If we are turned to God and to man in love, as Jesus instructs, it becomes impossible to hate other people, or even the labours of the day. The miracle is that when we are concentrated on the Lord like this, there is a corresponding transformation response from HIM. In mysterious, but absolutely practical ways, a new pattern is introduced into our minds and the old things, with their pains, are passed away. We begin to "dream our dreams with God", and our "dreams" come true!

We become attuned to the creative power of the universe, and the Divine order increasingly becomes established in our thinking, and new patterns produce new results. In fact, Divine Love transcends even the Law of Cause and Effect. Old causes are dissolved and the new dynamic of Love sweeps into all-embracing action in mind, body and the business of living.

The fears and frustrations only have foundation and power when we give our allegiance to these weaknesses. But when we turn to the Lord with trust and faith He takes charge, and Divine adjustments effortlessly flow into our lives. We are only afraid when we rely upon our own inadequacies. Who can fear anything once the truth of eternal life is accepted? Who can worry about any kind of problem, if we know the Reality of God's care and power, and that He is now in charge? Even the grief of separation, when a loved one goes home to the greater kingdom, dissolves in the compassion and strength of God as He gives the good news of new life for the one who has gone on to await our coming.

Our thoughts, consciously and sub-consciously, therefore

conform to the Divine Pattern, and we embark on the true journey of positive thinking and imagination in tune with the Lord's thinking. And herein is our Father glorified, in that He is the One Life awakening in us all, just as quickly as we become ready to accept it.

With all this in view we need to extend our vision, our imagination, and our receptivity to Divine ideas. We are now only interested in the leading of His Spirit, for we know that His will is now the inward and outward operative factor in our experience. Divine love radiates through the entire range of daily events, in our relationships with people, and in the creativeness which HE is now initiating. The all-pervading creative power is LOVE linked with IMAGINATION to provide the perfect patterns for corresponding outward achievement.

The practice of the Presence of God is a moment by moment aspiration. Like Brother Lawrence, the most humble cook in the monastery of old, we need to do all things and think all things as a constant service to the glory of God.

This is the *only* moment in which we can experience anything. This is our eternal life, here, now—even as you read these words. Yesterday has passed into the realm of memory, the next moment has not yet reached us. But *this moment* is vital, for it contains the very essence of life, and it conditions for good or ill the moment to follow, tomorrow, and all that lies ahead.

The more, therefore, we can become centred in Love and Faith NOW, the more surely will these blessings subsequently flow. As the unwary mind will constantly be tempted by the pressure of the outward scene to stray, this is one of the central secrets to hold in consciousness. We are with God NOW, in this moment, and Perfect Everything is in dynamic expression. Peace and harmony, in the Divine order, is NOW the true reality, no matter what the outward appearance may be.

Then, in this approach, it is the Father Who gives us strength and courage, and it is His spirit that is unfolding the highway into the future. In Him we behold the Perfection Pattern and know it to be Real, and thus learn to change outward disease or disaster by abiding in the inward Perfect Picture first. As within, so without.

This principle of God *here and now* is so important that we cannot emphasise it too strongly. The mind so easily leaps from the present moment, when under the pressure of pain and problem, to pattern ahead all kinds of possibilities, and thus prepare the way for worse troubles. We are told in the Good Book that the things we fear, or pattern, tend to come upon us.

In perfect faith we know that every experience is necessary for our eternal growth. We know that life is awakening every good in us, and distilling this by teaching us to use our love and faith in the face of every adversity. Only by matching our qualities with the difficulties can we discover the effectiveness of the Law.

In this sense, the entire range of what may be termed the problems of life—from sin to sickness, difficulties and disasters—invite us to arise and come closer to the Lord. And when we do so the way opens, sometimes instantaneously, sometimes over quite long periods of time.

Much true prayer is frustrated because we do not clearly understand the fact that life does not pass through *time*, but through moment-by-moment personal experience. We seldom pause to consider that countless problems, even when prayer is introduced, can only be solved through a succession of events which may involve many people, and many changes of character, or circumstances stretching through weeks or months.

The very nature of life decrees that it unfolds, or evolves, and that this must take place in ordered sequence, through our thinking and our fellowship with other people. Whatever difficulties come our way the same principle which produced them must be motivated, even through prayer, to bring about whatever changes are inherent in the Divine adjustment we now seek.

The moment we come into communion with God, in the way described herein, everything is released to Him. We should then know that every complicated aspect of life and its true needs are now moving through *every immediate moment* to a complete adjustment. It may not be completed for months, but day by day the practice of the Presence of God will reveal the progress made and the changes that are occurring. In other words, we must trust NOW, and constantly, to the end of every sequence.

We are in too big a hurry, because we can only feel the pain or see the problem, and do not scan the wider horizon of life and its real needs. We fervently pray today, give it all to the Lord, and then tomorrow clutch it all back from Him, as we return to our worries and self-effort again. We leave the Perfection Pattern, and re-set our pattern of imperfection with its corresponding complications.

* * * *

This brings into focus a prevailing attitude of mind which needs healing in most of us. As a race, we are thrilled when "good" things are happening, and distressed or worried when difficulties (of a thousand degrees of pain or intensity) meet us.

If we are going to live the Divine Thinking way with Christ, we shall need to learn that the so-called problems are equal in their virtue and importance, perhaps more so, to the experiences we describe as "good". These are the bricks with which we build the personal house of the kingdom within us. We should find it impossible to live at all if everything was on one flat plane of expression.

We live and grow within the framework of "opposites", and could have no measure of life were it not for "good" and "evil", light and shade, love and hatred, joy and sadness, and all the thousand variations which make us what we are. As co-heirs with Christ, we are really here to share in creation, and this involves taking the unformed experience and moulding something beautiful out of it.

An ugly situation invites us to transform it by love, prayer and fellowship. A block of marble may contain the angel of a sculptor's dreams, but he must work to chip away the unwanted stone before it can be revealed. These pages of foolscap on which I write would remain empty of words, if the vision of my mind was not allowed to express itself in concentrated day by day dedication, prayer and writing. Sickness invites our patient understanding of the central laws which govern our temporary residence in this physical temple of His spirit. Through the whole range of perceptions we are constantly learning the art of living, transmuting negative into positive experience.

We must all, therefore, learn not to rebel nor try to run away from these valuable gifts of the spirit. They are the stepping-stones to eternal life in the Divine Awakening.

If a man came to your door one day and said, "Good morning, Sir. Good morning, Madam. You see this barrow-load of wet mud balls? Well, I have been instructed to bring them to your house, and to tip them on to the carpet in your lounge. May I bring them in?" No doubt you, the gentle housewife, or even a mere man, would raise your hands and voice in astonished protest. "What—on my best carpet! Oh, no, not on your life! What is this madness? Take that filthy stuff away!"

But what would your reaction be if he then said:

"Just a moment please. I just wanted to tell you that this is an unconditional gift to you. Every ball of clay contains a beautiful diamond, and they all belong to you as soon as I drop them on your carpet!"

I guess you wouldn't be able to let him in quickly enough! In a few moments, all this muck and mire would be piled on your rich Chinese carpet, and your family would be on their knees eagerly scrabbling about in the mud. You would dash off to the kitchen to wash away the slime, bring back each shining diamond, and dig deep into the pile again for more.

Heedless of the lesser things like a lovely carpet, beautiful clothes and polished finger-nails, the supreme objective would be the recovery of the diamonds hidden in the clay!

Every difficulty, of whatever kind, is but a diamond encased in the mud, inviting us to probe for it.

Moment by moment, when poised in Divine love, we are taken through the full range of eternal ways, and become fulfilled in His Will and Purpose, as we pass along the successive stages of our pilgrimage.

This, therefore, is the scientific Christ Way for everyone, from the boy and girl at school to the businessman at the peak of his career. And none can afford to ignore this fundamental truth, for it has a profound and practical bearing upon every aspect of human life and its high destiny.

How inspired, indeed, are the words which reflect this realisation:

"Whatsoever things are true, whatsoever things are honest, whatsoever things are just, whatsoever things are pure, whatsoever things are lovely, whatsoever things are of good report; if there be any virtue, and if there be any praise, think on these things."

In the full context of its meaning, it is the Father Who makes it possible to do so. It takes us not only into the wider appreciation of the factors governing Divine healing, but far beyond it, into the prevention of disease and the wondrous way of life which is our true and natural inheritance.

It takes us also into a rich and rewarding fellowship with other people who pursue the same spiritual objectives. That is why church life and prayer groups offer such opportunities when we bring this kind of vision into realistic practice.

I remember once wandering quietly across the grassy glades in the redwood forest at a Camp Farthest Out retreat in the Santa Cruz mountains in California. It was prayer-group time, and in or under the redwood groves groups of people were in prayer.

These groups were designed to allow everyone to cultivate and express their own prayer consciousness, and we leaders just sat in wherever the Lord led us. It was a deep experience to move freely in this sacred atmosphere, and I became intensely aware of the Divine radiance emanating from each group.

Each time I quietly sat down in one of these groups, it was like coming out of a room into the sunshine. The Presence was tangibly Real.

Have you ever looked into the faces of people in prayer? There is probably no greater witness to all I have said than the remarkable transformation that takes place in us during a period of intercession. And, in a retreat organised to intensify this dedication, one knows without words that wonderful things are happening.

I have met hundreds of prayer groups down the years, of every denomination. And the Presence is always known to those who serve Him like this. It is the fulfilment of the age-old truth that when two or three are gathered together in the name of Jesus, He is in the midst of them.

Everything I have been guided to write in these pages could have been written specially for prayer groups. This is the kind of inspiration which can quicken their experience and speed them forward into the greatest work of this time.

Prayer groups are rapidly growing in number and potency, as individually and collectively people realise the importance of true discipleship. Now that we realise that prayer and Divine healing are the prerogative of *everyone* to express, entirely new vistas of potential open before those who are ready to see them.

The new revolution of the Christ Way will surely awaken in the individual, as he or she becomes committed. And this can be intensified when more and more people know they can begin a prayer group by simply meeting with one, two or more friends in their own home or in their church.

Today tape recordings are available to help such people and, so far as the World Healing Crusade is concerned, they can be obtained absolutely free of cost for the asking. We so firmly believe in the almost unexplored power inherent in every person, that we can only urge, inspire, and seek to help everyone to accept this bold venture of faith which leads to Divine Action.

In this sense, do not wait until you are spiritual enough, worthy enough, or even willing enough. Another simple truth about our fellowship with Christ is that if we all waited until we were worthy or good enough to serve our Lord, there would never be any service rendered at all.

He is willing to take us just as we are, which is more than the world will often do. He will accept the talent we can offer, and gladly transform and magnify it as quickly as we will allow Him to do so.

Let the well-spring of love once be opened and He will show you, as he did the fishermen disciples of old, just what He can do with a soul simple and honest enough to believe that His Strength covers our weakness. This is Grace indeed!

The work of prayer groups today and in the future will probably do more than most to open the way for all humanity to walk in love, peace and prosperity, because they gather in dedicated fellowship to test and prove it for themselves.

Whenever the prayer group is in session, it is always inspiring to realise that it is the Father Who is doing the work, and that He is doing it constantly through thousands of similar groups. God's Plans and Purposes are linked with a world-wide work, and it may well be your privilege to be part of the service initiated by Him for the well-being of all.

With love comes enthusiasm, interest and dedication. For there is no higher enterprise than that which thankfully acknowledges Christ by giving in service. There is no higher vision than a complete acceptance of the truth that it is the Lord Who stirs and moves you to serve Him.

"Ye have not chosen Me, but I have chosen you, and ordained you, that ye should go and bring forth fruit, and that your fruit should remain; that whatsoever ye shall ask of the Father in my name, he may give it you. . . .

"And ye also shall bear witness, because ye have been with me from the beginning". Jesus—to YOU!

It is, for you, for me, and for all, the Divine Awakening.

*   *   *   *

Thank you, Father, for the vision of all that we can accomplish in partnership with Thee. Help us Lord to be so truly dedicated that we may receive Thy Thoughts and thus unfold our lives in wondrous ways as directed by Thee. May we become Love in full expression and be the channel of infinite creativeness and blessing for the well-being of all. Amen.

New Vision

Pray for one another, that ye may be healed.

JAMES 5: 16.

HOWEVER MUCH WE MAY WISH to ignore it, the central fact still remains that thousands of people have been healed of apparently incurable disease by prayer. It is, indeed, the new vision of our age.

Since this touches the lives of us all, as it did when Jesus ministered and showed the way, it is illogical just to bury our heads in the sand and carry on as though nothing had happened.

In the end, the only real purpose behind every church is to help awaken a happier, healthier and more effective way of life. Inevitably, we are concerned for people, the individual "Mrs. Jones" or "Tom Smith", and what is actually happening to them. And this, as with Christ Himself, transcends buildings, organisations, methods or means.

At one service we had witnessed the Lord instantly and visibly healing a number of people. At the end, as the congregation dispersed, three men came to me and said, "You know, this is the work of the devil. You did not mention the Blood of the Lamb!" In spite of the fact that we had all been praying in the Name and Love of Jesus Christ!

Our terminology may differ, although we say the same things in other words. It is what is in our hearts that counts with the Lord and surely the essence of love is tolerance, understanding and freedom from judgment.

So the minister today seriously begins to consider the

significance and implication of Divine Healing. He wants the whole man perhaps even more than most other people. He yearns for the Christ as He must have appeared to the people of the young Church when every Christian was on fire with the Holy Spirit. Actually, he is held back more by the apathy and lack of faith in his congregation than by his own limitation. There is such a need for the people to see this new vision and to bring their own intensified love and faith to church. Any minister would soar to unprecedented heights on the encouragement, love and faith of his flock.

But he, too, can do much to stimulate this. After all, he has only to take Christ at His word and emphasise it with his own faith and conviction. It is wonderful how people respond to the full truth, and sad how easily they flag before a milk-and-water Christianity. The Christian tradition is one of good works, of mighty works, and no Christian can ever be happy until he is deeply involved in the production of them.

I met a Methodist minister at a Camp Farthest Out in Oklahoma, the Rev. Reginald Goff. He was aflame with the Holy Spirit, and so was his congregation. For one hour each day he told us the story of his "working church". And it was like listening to the Acts of the Apostles.

He was not reporting his own wonderful ministry, but telling the story of the healings, transformed lives and Divine adjustments which followed the work of his seventeen prayer groups! Seventeen prayer groups! Can you imagine it? There are thousands of churches today without even one prayer group, and they miss the greatest Light of all, for it can only come through people as they learn to pray and arise to be about the Father's business.

These groups were organised in teams of about ten to twelve people, with double that number when couples, a man and wife, formed the group. They not only prayed. They also went about, in the name of Christ, doing good works, visiting the sick, succouring the weak, the old and lonely. And, as he said, his church came alive with the joy, power and quickening Spirit of Christ from the moment prayer group work began.

Seeking the cause, and then bringing the sick friend before the Lord in repentance, forgiveness, faith and love must ever be the paramount objective of minister, and all who seek to help those in need. To this we need only add our own absolute assurance that something wonderful, visible or invisible, is happening. God is in action, in the right way, for the highest good of the person concerned.

There is no personal responsibility attaching to the minister in healing. He cannot heal anyone. But he can be the channel of love and faith, knowing that because the Father is there, only good can follow. His personal faith is the most potent way of helping the sick to go with him all the way to the Lord.

Healings take place in many ways. The traditional sacrament of anointing with oil, the laying on of hands, the communion service, and simple prayer are all equally effective. In our own ministry we have been led through the experience of all these ways, but now emphasise the teaching of committal, repentance, forgiveness and a complete adherence to the Christ Way of Love as the means of transmuting the cause of the trouble, and opening the way to the abundant life.

To this we add the prayer for awakening the whole man, for the healing of cause and effect, and that God's Will in Perfect Everything may now ensue, in the Name of Jesus Christ.

And it is a simple truth that many people become instantly healed through this comprehensive approach. Others are partially healed and then go forward to complete it in their own changed attitudes in personal communion with God. Others are apparently not healed physically, but I have never met anyone yet who was not strengthened spiritually, mentally and emotionally through prayer. In fact, there is no such thing as unanswered prayer. God always responds and gives to us just what is right, and what we can accept, as He leads us ever onward into the Light.

We believe in seeking only to realise the presence of God, and quietly to wait upon Him, poised in His peace, centred in His perfection. We think it better not to whip up the emotions, but rather to abide in the Father, praying and believing. It is better, however, not to dogmatise, judge or condemn any method of coming to the Father, because He has ways which we know very little about.

I recall, for example, a week on a mission in Belgium, under the auspices of the Pentecostal Church. I had flown in from Amsterdam, and the plane was a little late. When we arrived at the church it was crowded to capacity, and there was a pandemonium of voices shouting their praise to God.

Accustomed, as I am, to conducting services in the Great Peace of the Presence, my feelings were very mixed and somewhat shattered as I took my place to lead the service. As it proceeded, amidst the prevailing noise, blended with my English, the interpreter's Flemish, and the babble of foreign tongues talking individually to God, I became aware of a wondrous Power in our midst.

During this service, and every day for a week, I do not think I have ever seen so many people healed by prayer. They had come for that purpose, and they received what they expected. As I moved about among them, praying in English, there was no longer any need for an interpreter. Christ simply took charge and the healings followed.

They were busy days, because the pastor took me on day-long visits to sick people who could not come to the service. At one house, as we entered, there was the usual pandemonium of worship. It was about 10.30 a.m., but about forty people, still on their knees when we went in, had been there since 7 a.m. in prayer for a man who had lain for years paralysed from head to foot on the bed under the window of this large room!

Prayer, however formulated, will move mountains. I went to the man on the bed, talked a little and then prayed, backed by the fervent ejaculations of the forty intercessors. When leaving, there was apparently no change in the sick man.

The lady of the house gave me a little vase as a memento.

I found later that it had been left behind, so asked the pastor to take me back later in the day to retrieve it.

As we walked up the garden path, the door burst open and framed in it was the wife and the man who had been paralysed! They said that as soon as all the people had left, the husband simply got out of bed, dressed himself and was perfectly whole.

But forty people gave up their time and work, and came to pray!

The more we consider the facts of Divine healing as revealed by the thousands of case histories, the more surely must we see that inherent in this experience is a new dimension of being, full of vital potentials and possibilities for the well-being of the entire race. If we are failing to experience these benedictions throughout the social structure, this can only mean that we are not, in some way, using the Laws which govern this release of Divine Action.

Once the reality of a Law of such potency has been discovered and used, anything may happen, and though we appear to fail such failure is due to our lack of knowledge or mis-use of His law and not to anything in God. There can be no fault or failure in Him.

The present position is that many people, and many ministers, have confirmed that prayer can work wonders, even as Jesus revealed. This fact is the most vital discovery of modern times and, through the abundant testimony, it should already have stimulated the most intensive research and mass application of known principles. It should have swept through the Church and medical profession as the beginning of a new exploration into a realm of being with infinite possibilities.

Every minister, and countless other people, have had examples of answered prayer. We reiterate that, fundamentally, Divine healing and prayer are linked together, and should never be segregated by a concept that prayer is one factor in life, and Divine healing isolated in "gifts of healing" possessed by a few special people.

This latter idea has probably halted our full experience of Divine healing more than anything else. We got lost because we did not fully understand the healing work of Jesus, or the biblical statement that some are given "gifts of healing".

It is true that, through recorded history, we have had among us people who had the unique ability to bring healing to others. They have always been labelled "Healers". They have worked under many concepts and titles. Some give their total allegiance to Christ in prayer; some are psychic healers and believe they work with God and a ministry of heavenly beings; others just have a compulsion to heal, without much knowledge of the laws, except that it transcends ordinary experience.

But all these people, without exception, are exercising their faith in God, in His responding power to heal, and are united in their love for humanity—a yearning to help people in trouble. And it has been demonstrated beyond the slightest shadow of doubt that the Father transcends the differences of dogma, creed or approach when faith and love are opened unto Him.

As we seek to work in the Christ Love, there is a salutary lesson for us all in this observable fact. It clearly shows us that we fail Him when we become earthbound by judging others who serve in ways differing from our own. It is a transcendental fact that anyone who receives healing through any agency also becomes spiritually awakened in the process. There is no surer way of turning a man's mind to God than to demonstrate His care for us in a "rescue operation", removing some dreadful disease or disaster.

All these people are motivated by high spiritual aspiration and are responding to the aspect of spiritual truth they know. The world calls them "healers" because their lifework is centred in this expression. But it only came into being because they were inspired to use the spiritual laws which belong to every living soul.

The "gifts of healing" meant only that, as in the preaching ministry, certain people would be called to reveal the truth in that direction. On this particular level of effectiveness they are still exponents of the love and faith which make communion with God possible, and whatever concepts they personally follow, these central qualities, in varying degrees of expression, govern their healing experience. It is the Father who heals, and the prerogative of everyone to pray for others regardless of label.

Through the work of many modern disciples, the Christian Church is increasingly adopting the Christ Way in healing. It is focused mainly in ministers who have seen the significance of the teaching of Jesus about the effectiveness of prayer, and the spiritual principles which are essential to the well-being of the *whole* man.

Without exception, right through the Christian Church, all these enlightened leaders point to the Healing Love of Christ, effective through faith and prayer. The logical result has been the formation of countless prayer groups giving "ordinary" people the opportunity to use the same principles for healing, and the works have followed, according to the degree these qualities were exercised.

The greatest revelation of the age has been that the true secret of Divine Healing lies in the full Christian precept, and that it is the birthright and prerogative of all, as Jesus taught. "Pray for one another that ye may be healed." "The effectual prayer of a righteous man availeth much."

And, after all, throughout the Gospels, it is Jesus Himself Who persistently instructs us to pray. "Seek ye first the Kingdom of God (to know the Presence of Perfection) and its righteousness (His Love), and all these things (the healing and things we need) shall be added unto you." "What things soever ye desire, when ye pray, *believe that ye receive them,* and ye shall have them."

The Church stands in a remarkable position in the light of the Gospels and the modern confirmation of the truth through healing. She offers the fundamental and comprehensive approach to the whole man—spiritually, mentally, physically

and materially—which is a vision transcending physical healing as such.

Too often in the past the emphasis, through "gifts of healing" held to be the prerogative of the few, has been on
physical healing as the main objective. Due primarily to the
research work in the field of Divine Healing the Christ Way,
and the rapidly accumulating scientific evidence of the psychologist and doctor, we know full well the need to sublimate
and heal the spiritual-mental-emotional cause of disease before
a completely effective approach can be made to the healing of
a large percentage of physical sickness.

Therefore, with new courage and faith, the Christian
Church as a whole has a confirmed foundation from which
she can boldly leap into leadership, and provide an authority
and practice which everyone yearns to experience.

The ministry and congregations have held a living truth in
their midst for nearly two thousand years. It is time to blow
the cobwebs away and bring this treasure into virile circulation. It is the only doctrine which embraces the full possibility
of healing cause and effect, and which gives us the vision
that man's spiritual and eternal needs are of first importance.
Then, with Jesus, we can confidently expect Divine Order to
ensue. The other things will be added unto us.

Once we begin to consider seriously the possibility of
communion with God, we must naturally lift our vision to
seek at least a comprehension of the magnitude of such
aspiration and experience. In the past, it would seem that
even if we have not made our God too "little", we have
certainly not expected very big works to follow our consulta-
tion with Him.

Our faith must match the fact of communion, and embrace
the reality of the absolute Perfection which should be our
high expectation in surrender and prayer. And, if we have
our being in His spirit, we not only need to know the
simplicity of immediate contact, but also extend our vision to
realise that all people, and all creation, are also centred in
Him.

This opens an infinite horizon to our inward perception. It brings into focus our essential unity with all life. And it helps the little human personality to arise out of the prison of self to experience a deeper understanding of the Almighty Nature of God.

For example, the recognition of the truth that all are one in Him made possible the tremendous advance in absent, or distant healing. In so many ministries today, including our own, teaching and prayer extend to countless people whom we never see personally. And now the weight of accumulated evidence is so powerful that nobody can afford to ignore the significance of these "mighty works" of the Lord through prayer.

It is wonderful what prayer can do, but it is certainly not limited to healing. Its greater scope is in creativeness and the achievement of every kind of good objective for human well-being. I remember, for example, the tremendous prayer project of Dr. John Hinkle of the Christ Unity Church in Sacramento, California.

When he became the minister of this church, he had a yearning to help old people. He felt that the general approach to the problems of age in providing institutions was quite inadequate, and had a vision for a perfect establishment which would enable every member not only to be cared for, but to feel needed by the community.

He realised that so many people, forced by circumstances to retire from active life, were in fact still pulsing with an accumulated lifetime's experience and knowledge, which was often immediately blocked on retirement. He felt their need for interesting expression and continued service to the community. He was inspired with the idea to build a block of modern apartments and chalets in extensive grounds to house old people, and to provide every conceivable kind of activity to match the creative desires of the occupants. He wanted to help them form panels of professional consultants to channel wisdom and knowledge into the community, so that they could not only continue to serve, but feel needed. And in many ways he dreamed his dream, and *prayed*.

One day he described the project to his congregation and asked for their prayers. Shortly afterwards, a woman was walking alongside a country site, and the Lord told her to put a deposit on it. Dr. Hinkle now had a piece of ground—I think he said forty-five acres. And the people went to the site and prayed. Soon it was a hundred acres!

Thereafter, in many wonderful ways, architects, engineers, city planners, legal advisers, draughtsmen all came to him with offers of help. An intensive research across the entire national field of old age problems was instituted and, after four years, equipped with comprehensive building plans and all data necessary to the perfect objective, he is in the midst of a five-million-dollar project!

Prayer breeds big ideas when we are really prepared to go far and wide with God in the love that yearns to heal and serve. The Law of Love was fulfilled, and my soul thrilled to hear it, when he told me that all their plans and research data were freely available to any other church or organisation desiring to do the same.

*   *   *   *

Thus we see prayer ranging from Divine Healing in a church, healing across thousands of miles, to the awakening of a great vision for advancing the well-being of elderly people. Prayer is comprehensive. It should, and can, cover every aspect of life from sickness to the highest achievements we can conceive to be true to our nature.

In the light of the true Christ vision, how thankfully we can rejoice whenever we see labourers striding boldly into the fields of life to gather in the harvests that are so ripe! Every such worker, of every denomination, quickens the power of the whole. The barriers are rapidly falling, divisions are evaporating, as we see only the ONE work of the Lord and can thankfully offer one's own church to the common cause. When millions of new workers in prayer arise in Christ in all our churches, we shall swiftly move into the abundant life for which everyone in the world inwardly yearns.

There is great power in fellowship in every kind of project. In fact, everything man ever accomplished is done in partnership with other people. Likewise in prayer. There is nothing more potent than a congregation united in prayer for Divine healing.

Sometimes individual ministers decree that Divine healing, if attempted at all, should be done personally and not in public. I agree that there is always the need for personal help, and every minister spends a vast amount of time guiding individual members of his community. But I disagree completely that Divine healing in public worship can either harm anyone or cause any lack of faith.

When many people in church are inspired to love and serve in prayer, with faith, the Presence of God is experienced by all. And it is impossible to be in His presence and not be blessed in some way for our highest good.

It is also significant that most of the Divine healing revealed by Jesus Himself, and the early disciples and Christians, was accomplished in the midst of great gatherings. If this was the Christ Way, I do not think anyone can presume to declare we can do better than emulate His example. In modern Divine healing services, I would only suggest that the actual Healing Prayer Service should always be preceded by spiritual teaching, to remind us of the importance of repentance, forgiveness, love, faith and the complete surrender of our lives to Him.

Certain it is that thousands of people have been healed by God at public services who would have continued to be sick, bruised or broken had they not attended. Who can dare to tell the Lord how He shall work? Every single life is important to Him. Rather than obstruct any channel of love and faith, we should all work together to multiply the entire experience in the widest and most comprehensive way possible.

As one of so many examples which illustrate this statement,

here is the tape-recorded witness of Mrs. Wallace, who was healed at such a service in the Metropolitan Methodist Church at Cape Town: —

"I attended your Divine healing service in the Metropolitan Church. My husband came home one day with your pamphlet about the services that were going to take place here. At the bottom of that pamphlet you had a testimony of a lady who had been healed of a slipped disc in her spine. I had a slipped disc in my neck. I'd been to hospital where they stretched it and I left wearing a brace. My husband came home and said to me, 'Look at this. Don't you think this a direct lead for you?'

"So I started thinking about it. In the house we had a book called *The Healing Light** by Agnes Sanford. I hadn't bothered about reading it. My husband had read it, and it was lying around. I now felt I had to read this book. So a friend of mine gave me an apparatus to hold it up while I read it. As I was reading it, I thought to myself, 'You know, you've been wrong. You've always prayed negatively. You must pray positively, believing that God *is* healing you.'

"Well, I came to your service. As I walked into the church, I just felt that tonight I was going to be healed. I felt the presence of the Lord there. Previous to that I hadn't been able to sit still. I had to move around, but while you were giving your message I don't think I moved. All pain was removed from me.

"When you walked down the aisle my heart felt as though it was pushing my chest walls completely out. I just couldn't breathe—I didn't know what to do with myself. And when you asked us to stand up I stood there gasping for breath. I think it was as though electricity was going through me from the tips of my toes right up to my head.

"I stood there, and when you came up to me you asked

*Published by Arthur James, Ltd.

me what was wrong. I said I had a slipped disc. Then you told me about the lady who was healed in East London. I listened to you, but while you were speaking I thought, 'Well, I'm going to get rid of the steel cage and brace round my head and neck.' I took it off. I was compelled to do it. I thought, 'God is healing me. God *has* healed me. Why do I want this on my neck?' So I took it off and put it down.

"And when you asked me to go to the Communion rail, I fell down there on my knees. The relief was so great that I broke down completely, I just sobbed, and praised God and thanked Him for healing me. When I got home, I put the cage contraption on top of the wardrobe, and haven't needed it since. I now do all my own housework, the washing, and everything. My neck was perfectly healed."

As I have said, this dramatic testimony of healing has been recorded and so is available to those who would care to hear this woman's actual voice. For myself I believe this is just one more concrete example of Christ's Healing Ministry on earth *today*. This woman, as we all are, was important to God and because she was receptive to His promptings she came to the church where the praying community lifted her trouble to the Lord. And He answered!

So the true working Church is born through dedicated people in prayer. And prayer inevitably leads us into the Stillness as we wait upon the Lord.

It is at such moments as we listen to God that we think of Him, listen to His promptings and enter into the mystery of mystical meditation. Perhaps you would care to share some of my thoughts which have come to me at such treasured moments.

*   *   *   *

Thank You, Father, *for Thy Living Church, through Jesus Christ Our Lord.*

Thank You, Lord, for Thy Grace and Guidance extended to all Thy ministers and followers on earth, and for the love which illumines their dedicated lives. And thank You for the new vision which is dawning everywhere.

We pray for them all, that they may be inspired with ever greater vision and be so united in Christ that they may indeed lead all mankind into the freedom and peace of this New Christ Age.

May all Thy children everywhere be stirred in every congregation to arise as Thy disciples and thus reveal the works and wonders of the Christ Way. And, in simple love and committal, please use each of us now to take our part in fulfilling this New vision.

Thank You, Father. Amen.

I I

Secrets of the Silence

*She is more precious than rubies; and all the things thou
canst desire are not to be compared unto her. Her ways
are ways of pleasantness, and all her paths are peace.*

PROVERBS 3: 15, 17.

THE LATE HENRY THOMAS HAMBLIN, founder
and editor of the *Science of Thought Review*, Bosham
House, Chichester, England, was one of the most
remarkable mystics of modern times.

Through his lifework of meditation, the world-known
magazine, and many books, the Lord used him as a Light to
shine in countless dark lives, and to illumine a pathway
along which so many churches, organisations and people now
march.

His central concept was consistently centred on the practising of the Presence of God. Throughout his long life—he
passed into the higher life at eighty-six—he talked and wrote
about the Silence, the abiding in the Perfection of the Lord.
He was probably the greatest exponent of meditation in the
land, and certainly spent his days practising it himself.

I first began to be aware of him some time after the Lord
opened my first Sanctuary. Someone gave me a copy of the
Science of Thought Review, and as I read his illumined words
I felt an immediate bond with him. He was speaking the
same language of love and faith and peace which had suddenly become the central flame of my own life.

Shortly afterwards his book *A Venture of Faith* came to me,
bringing such comforting confirmation that the way I was
seeking to go with Jesus had already been safely journeyed by
Mr. Hamblin himself and by the German Pastor Muller

about whom this book was written. It told how this penniless pastor founded and maintained one of the biggest orphanages in the world at Bristol, England, entirely through love, faith and prayer. And in all this he never, ever, asked one penny from anybody. He simply prayed, believing, and the right things happened, in the right way and at the right time to bring into being this vast enterprise—which still stands today as a living monument to his trust.

I remember one of the stories he told about Muller concerned an acute food problem. The larders were empty and there was not enough for all the children's breakfast. The pastor prayed. At breakfast time he began to assemble all his charges for the meal, just as though the outward abundance was there as usual. And, as he did so, a van from a local grocery store drew up laden with provisions.

The owner of the store said he had been awakened very early by a Presence and a Voice, which asked him to fill his van with food and take it to the orphanage.

These were the things the beloved Henry Thomas Hamblin also believed and practised all his life.

I longed to meet him, but had already grown accustomed to the conviction that in all things, the Father would arrange it if and when necessary. And the time came when, quite exceptional to his way of serving, Mr. Hamblin accepted an invitation—unknown to me at the time—to take the chair at a service I was to conduct in the Caxton Hall, London.

I was delighted when the news came and eagerly looked forward to the event. As I went into the ante-room for my customary hour of meditation before the service, it was impossible not to speculate on what we would talk about. Fifteen minutes later Mr. Hamblin came in. Elderly, broad-built, high forehead—a handsome face with a little beard—and Peace. We shook hands, looked eye to eye, and he said, "Let's go into the Silence!"

So we communed with the Father in the Great Stillness, and knew more about each other than all the words that we could ever have spoken.

In the service he led the whole congregation into the Silence too! Very few words were spoken, and in these he only described the glow of God's Presence in which we had both been poised earlier. It was a tremendous service.

Thereafter, when opportunity offered and I was travelling that way, I would drop in to see him and his beloved wife. She was somewhat older than he, but always radiant and full of energy. They lived near Chichester on the south coast, and his home and offices were in the midst of a garden of trees and flowers. And, always, our main communion was in the Silence.

Once I had been exceptionally busy after a week of intensive work, two services each day and a lot more besides, and was travelling west for another week in that direction. Somehow I felt very depleted, which is not customary with me, especially when taking services, which always refresh and invigorate. However, I called on the Hamblins for an hour en route.

Mr. Hamblin was in his office sitting in the Silence. He looked up as I entered. "Come and join me," he said. So we went into the Stillness. And wave after wave of wondrous energy flooded into me. An hour later I resumed my journey, completely renewed in every way.

How good it is that his teaching will never be lost, because the *Science of Thought Review* carries on the work, and every month bears Henry Thomas Hamblin's mystical thoughts, reprinted from the writings of a lifetime.

It is a steadying thought to realise that so great a work could have had so wide an influence emanating, as it did, from one man spending so much time in the Silence, waiting upon the Lord. He seldom went away from the precincts of his home and office. It was the Lord Who did the "travelling" and the work. And the people who were ready for his vision beat a pathway to his door.

The world has been blessed indeed because Henry Thomas Hamblin passed through it.

The mystery of the Great Silence has exercised the minds of men down the ages. I believe it to be fundamental to our highest communion with God, and now I would like to offer you some more observations and experiences in meditation.

*　　*　　*　　*

We are an impatient generation, and have been taught in many ways that positive action, following clear positive thinking, is the best way to achieve anything in this world. We are confirmed in this by the fantastic array of products pouring through the thought system in every land. The prosperity we know proclaims the power of our thinking, and it goads us on to ever greater cultivation of mental power and corresponding activity.

But we only know in part. "When I was a child I spake as a child, I understood as a child, I thought as a child: but when I became a man, I put away childish things . . .

"And now abideth faith, hope, love, these three; but the greatest of these is love."

It is true that imagination, will power and all thought will produce their equivalents in outward expression as surely as the sun will always cast a shadow. But there is a superior kind of thinking which can produce changes of such dynamic quality that, when we know about it, we wonder how we could have been so childish for so long.

We find this kind of thinking, and corresponding creativeness, in the Silence, thinking God's Thoughts after Him.

In Proverbs 3, we are told in poetic and profound language exactly what will happen if we closely follow the instructions given to us about our relationship with the Lord. Every soul on earth would like to possess every aspect of what is promised here, but it would seem that the vast majority do not really believe such treasures exist in this way, so do not bother to follow the directions which would lead us to them.

It is as though we were starving to death because we had no money, when there is a hoard of gold buried a foot deep in the back garden. A man says, "Why are you starving when I know there is gold in your garden?" The starving one replies, "Oh, don't bother me—I've heard fairy stories like that before.

I wouldn't waste my energy in even digging in a place where I have seen the grass growing since I was a boy."

The Bible gives us instructions from beginning to end, and repeats them in a thousand ways of emphasis—in poetry, parable and proof. As Jesus said : "If ye abide in me, and my words (my instructions) abide in you, ye shall ask what ye will, and it shall be done unto you."

Every kind of experience, with its inward and outward manifestations, can only follow the faith and application we give to it. We would not even expect to enjoy the delights of a picnic on a mountain top unless we made the journey. We cannot know the soul-satisfying power inherent in music, art, love, a church service, or even a sunset, unless we give our attention and time. In fact, we spend our lives, moment by moment, observing, reacting and thinking about whatever is engaging our interest.

Incessantly, we select and implement the patterns of our thought stream and we march through life, not in time, but along the "stepping stones" of our thoughts, awareness, and corresponding events. And the pathways we initiate are as numerous as there are people on earth, or in heaven, to create them. We can lay our paths in jungles of sin and ignorance, or set them towards the mountain tops of our highest spiritual dreams.

The mystics tell us of the inward Light, the Peace of the Power of God, of Love and Fulfilment. They point to Divine Order, and illustrate how identification with Christ leads to an equivalent Order in our own lives. They know the deeper truths of inward and outward healing, and link the unfolding pathway with God's guidance. Their vision expands to comprehend the Oneness of all life and our personal communion with it through the spirit. They invariably witness to the truth that man's real goal is his union with the Lord in the inner kingdom, with all other things added. And they discover these truths in the Great Silence, being still before God.

It all springs from the worship which centres in surrendering the self completely to the Father. And this means, comprehensively, the acceptance of the Reality of the "invisible" Being of God, His infinite Love, Wisdom and Intelligence, and a corresponding desire that only His Will may be reflected through every thought, word and deed.

We learn to know that no matter what our personal desires may be, or our shrinking from any situation which faces us, our only real need is this trust in Him that everything may conform to the Lord's knowledge of our highest good. Jesus, when moving towards the culminating crisis of the Cross, prayed in the Garden of Gethsemane to confirm His awareness of God's Purpose irrespective of personal feelings:

> "Father, if thou be willing, remove this cup from me: nevertheless not my will, but thine, be done. And there appeared an angel unto Him from heaven, strengthening him" (Luke 22: 42, 43).

And thus, out of what the world would judge to be the ultimate disaster came the Resurrection and the consummation of all the needs of mankind.

The Love of Jesus was awakened in the Silence as He re-identified Himself with the Father. The real miracle of His Incarnation was that He came as a man, born not as a king, but as a babe in the lowliest of surroundings, and the son of humble parents. He came as a man, needing to pass through all the problems and difficulties we all have to meet.

He could have come as God, shining in Glory from the beginning, and in this Light could have made the Roman Empire bow before Him. He could have swept away the sin and sickness of the world in the simple action of Almighty Power released to demonstrate the fact "I Am God".

But He came as a man, humbly, simply, to live as we have to live, and thus revealed the heights and depths of a love which knew the secret of free will and the eternal Plan, designed to show His family how to awaken in personal awareness of the Power and Presence vested in the life of everyone.

The subsequent testimony of countless people who gave their allegiance and time to abiding in Him speaks with authority about the reality of such communion. It is as factual and practical as, on another level, is our recognition of the reality of our own lives and the way we follow day by day.

Therefore, these mystics point, through their personal awakening, to a dimension of awareness and action which transcends ordinary consciousness and brings into recognition and practice the high creative Power of God in human affairs. They are reporting the inward Reality of the Spirit, and describing the corresponding results of spending time being still in meditation.

To many this is an "intangible" realm indeed. The outward scene exerts a constant pressure which seems to prove its absolute reality, and we find it difficult to keep in focus the truth that it is the inward Power which makes and evolves everything.

People constantly ask about the technique of meditation. Many books have been written about it, but I still do not think of meditation as an involved method, which has to be taught like mathematics or some other subject.

Rather is there a need for deep simplicity, arising from a committal to the fact of God's Spirit here, now and always. I feel, intuitively, that we can obstruct rather than help by suggesting a mass of rules or steps. This is not to say that the many suggestions made by so many teachers have failed to help, because anything that turns the mind to God must be effective in some way.

But there is a "short cut", once we recognise that there is only God, and that each of us has a particular and unique entry into the awareness of His spirit already implanted by Him. We live in His Spirit. It is more His desire to draw us more closely into His own nature that provides the method, because He institutes it in the way that is intensely personal to us and our needs.

We sit "at the feet" of a preacher and pay attention. We should sit "at the feet" of the Master and KNOW the truth that makes us free. Then HE provides the teaching and moves far and wide across the scene of the environment to move people and events as necessary to unfold the Divine Pattern so far as it concerns us. Following this degree of surrender to God's Will, we are in the right place, at the right time, experiencing the motivating action of God designed to distil in us His Perfection, with eternal objectives ever in mind.

Most people become aware of a "stillness" that is not of this world when they seriously begin to give regular time to this practice. Jesus spoke much about the Peace and it is, indeed, the peace that passeth all understanding, because it is different from any other kind of peace. Words can certainly not describe it. We can only enter into personal awareness of it and thus know it for ourselves.

When our understanding embraces and accepts this sign of Peace as the Spirit now revealed, and that we are being "melted, moulded and filled" by It, then we come to appreciate the Stillness of the being of God. It is, truly, a state of Divine Order, of Peace, in which every outward thing is poised, balanced and expressed.

When we become still before God like this we are lifted above human effort as such, although His Power will flow through and strengthen our subsequent thoughts and actions. The entire concept of meditation is the giving of our being to God without straining or struggling to reach Him. We simply rest, or abide, in Perfection as simply as we abide in our bodies, sit in the sunshine, or allow music to impinge upon our senses. Essentially we accept, as fact, that the Lord is ministering unto us, NOW. We are limited only by the degree of our love, faith and acceptance of His Power.

Like every other important aspiration, progress is marked by the interest, time and attention we devote to the project. One trembles to think how much discord and disease there is in the world because we are too busy to pray like this. Reasonably enough, we cannot expect to find the Peace of Perfection unless we present ourselves to it, any more than we can hope to listen to a symphony concert by shutting ourselves up in a sound-proof room.

Many who have become trained in meditation sense an-inward rhythm which deepens the breathing. As we abide, an inward "breathing" seems to be induced, slower and deeper than usual, and this often then becomes a very gentle ebb and flow, linked with a feeling of being poised in this Peace.

I would in no way suggest this as a technique. If it occurs, it will have to do with the movement of the Spirit. It always happens to me; and so many people I have met, including Mr. Hamblin, find this is a sign of communion beginning, almost as though a door of the soul were being opened.

Jesus spent forty days and forty nights with God in the Silence. And His life was made One with the Father again. I wonder what would happen across the world scene, and throughout the Christian Church, if everyone even spent one hour each day like this? I am absolutely sure, even if everyone only paused two or three times a day in such silent communion, that the entire race would be swept straight into the new Christ Age far faster than all the progress we have made in this materialistic evolution.

The greatest moments I ever know are these times poised in the Peace. Before every service, the sole objective is to get self out of the way by coming reverently before Him, seeking only His Love and Presence, so that He can direct the meeting. I would tremble indeed if I had to take any service relying on my own mentality or personality. In fact, in my case, without prior meditation it would be impossible.

*   *   *   *

There is another aspect of Peace, this inward Stillness, which is only now beginning to be more widely and scientifically understood.

Modern knowledge reveals very clearly that tensions of every kind, broadly inherent in negative attitudes or compulsions, from sin to worry, are all states of discord, the opposite of Peace. Disease in the body represents, in ways known or unknown, something that is no longer in the balanced harmony of health. All the wars in history record the chaos reflected through the mass consciousness. And, in a thousand ways, the stresses and strains so prevalent in a modern society stem from a basic lack of Peace at the centre of the individual, group, nation or world family.

The opposite quality to any kind of tension, however expressed, is Peace. This realisation opens an entirely new perspective in the solution of the countless personal, national and international problems which, in greater or lesser degree, beset us all.

Wedded, as we are, to scientific concepts of every kind we can at least appreciate with our intellects the truth of these statements. Anybody knows that in Peace there is no tension, but as a race we have been frustrated because we have never considered deeply enough where to find such peace.

We have taken it as far as we can when, as in sickness, a doctor may advocate plenty of sleep or rest. And, surely enough, this is a great help. When a man is strained through overwork the same advice is given, and a restoration takes place. But there are countless aspects of life where even rest is not enough to heal or solve the problem. A war, for example, with its dreadful chaos, does not melt before sleep therapy.

We only go part of the way, and have not seriously considered the importance or even the reality of a Peace which has to do with the harmonies and equilibrium of Divine Order embracing all creation, from a nebula of stars a million light-years away to the mind and every cell in a human body here on earth.

The next scientific step forward in ecclesiastical, political, economic and educational research must certainly embrace this concept, because the incessant search for solutions will inevitably lead us into this other degree of Peace in which they surely lie.

And the individual, as he or she becomes awakened to this truth, can proceed immediately to practise it, without waiting for the ponderous deliberations of authorities still lost in their antiquated belief of their own ability to lift life up by its own shoe strings.

The Church, too, has a great opportunity and responsibility

in this direction, which is absolutely true to every aspect of her teaching and authority. She can assume a leadership in this prerogative that is already given into her keeping, and boldly open the way to the weary millions who still wander in the wilderness.

It is significant that many people are healed, for example, in Divine healing services while they are abiding in the Silence before God. They are, literally, exposed during this time to Divine Perfection, as surely as they would be exposed to sunshine when sitting in it. In a service devoted to healing their love, faith and prayer faculties are quickened, and people accordingly become more expectant of Christ's ministration.

Once we break away from the belief in "gifts of healing" as such, the "exclusive" prerogative of the dedicated individuals who seek to show how God's Love works, we can immediately begin to extend our own faith to a Father Who is present always, everywhere, and within our own beings. We then begin to look to God exclusively for our deliverance, and place our expectancy in our personal communion and in the prayers of others who commune with us. Our entire attention is thus centred on God, not man, no matter how great a "channel" we may believe him to be, being only thankful for the wonderful help he gives us in love, instruction and prayer.

In this approach we follow the teaching and prayer of the minister, prayer group or intercessor, but give our entire being into the direct action of God. We abide in the Father, and all His ways are Peace and Perfection, of which we partake.

Then we can really find the Living Presence in our churches. Millions of loving, dedicated and utterly sincere Christians give a tremendous allegiance to Christ and to their Church. But very few of us, relatively speaking, expect mighty works of healing, the solution of grave problems, and the awakening of a wondrous way of life in every way, to follow our attendance at the morning service.

We have not been fully taught to expect these things and therefore do not experience them, because our faith only makes real to us what we believe to be happening. If we had a cancer, for instance, very few people would believe that the *first best step* would be to sit in the congregation of their church in God's Presence. Yet this, in its highest sense, when fully understood and accepted, is exactly what should take place.

We come to church to be with the Lord, and to worship Him. What, therefore, should we expect to happen to us if we are immersed in the Spirit which is filling every part of the temple, including our own minds and bodies?

It would seem that we all need to stir our imagination, love and faith to realise the true nature of presenting ourselves to Him in the church we attend. All He needs from us is our faith and love, then even as we become poised in His Spirit, wonderful things will be happening to us.

We must expand our vision to meet the Lord Who could heal a thousand sick people simultaneously, in mass healing, if each one of them could reach the degree of receptivity, love and belief which exposed them to absolute Perfection. At this time we are not likely, as a community, to reach such heights, but every time we practise it we shall certainly move more surely into this awareness, and many will be healed and helped in the process.

In this sense, every service in every church is already a Divine Healing experience. We come before God to be spiritually awakened, to be forgiven our sins, to be purified in mind, body and affairs, so that we can follow Him into every necessary experience as we go back into the world.

When we teach this to our congregation, and inspire their faith to be still in God as they worship, then indeed shall we see a repetition of the fervour and mighty works which so startled the world through the common people of the early Church.

It leads us, too, into an even higher purpose in communion with the Lord. It takes us into effectual fervent prayer for one another, based on this same degree of faith and love: and, ultimately, leads us into the Peace where we wait upon the

Lord as a channel which HE proceeds to use to help people, situations and world events which He knows about.

We do not often consider the possibility of Jesus praying through us. We know about the possibility of our own prayers, but seldom think that HE might want to use our spiritual awakening to initiate prayer and power to circumstances of His choosing.

You can prove this for yourself. Be still, and ask the Lord to use you in any way He desires. Ask Him to bring to your attention the names of people and Divine objectives.

Then, as you rest in the Silence, listening, you will be aware of events and people, perhaps on a world-wide scale, with a sure feeling that they are made known to you by the Father, and not by your own thinking.

Be careful not to become involved in words of prayer or thought about the person or problem in your mind. Listen. And on realising the situation, simply whisper in your mind "Thank You, Father", accepting completely that the Blessing He wanted to initiate through you is now in operation. Then you are immediately ready for the next project, which is sealed by your "Thank You, Father"—and so on.

This is a very high form of meditation, especially as it is centred in love through service. You will soon be aware that the Lord is using you, and there can be no greater stimulus to our spiritual perception and aspiration than to have direct knowledge of it. And, of course, it keeps our minds stayed upon Him without effort or "mind wandering". We are with our Lord, and all is well.

"Her ways are ways of pleasantness, and all her paths are peace."

*   *   *   *

I become still . . . *in the Spirit of God. All tension ebbs away from me* . . . *Peace* . . . *the deep, still Peace of God enfolds me.* . . .

I am poised in the Peace of Perfect Everything and now rest in Thy Spirit. Thy Love glows through my being and I am one with Christ, now.

It is the Father Who takes my life and moulds it in the image and likeness of Christ. I believe.

Be still . . . be still . . . be still . . . in the Peace which passeth understanding. It is the Peace of God which is Perfection . . . now and for ever.

Now I am one with Thee, my Lord. Please use me as an instrument of love and faith to release Thy Perfection to people and world problems which You know are in need of Thy Power. As You bring them into my recognition, I thankfully acknowledge that wonderful Blessings are manifested according to Thy Will. I listen to Thee, Lord:

My friend . . . Thank You, Father.
Every Church . . . Thank You, Father.
The United Nations . . . Thank You, Father.
My Minister . . . Thank You, Father.*

In Thy Stillness You make known to me everything You desire me to share in prayer, through Jesus Christ our Lord. Amen.

* I offer these only as examples of prayer projects. God will reveal those appropriate to you as you listen to Him in the Silence.

12

This Day Will Dawn

> *That they all may be one; as thou, Father, art in me,
> and I in thee, that they also may be one in us; that the
> world may believe that thou hast sent me.*
>
> *And the glory which thou gavest me I have given
> them; that they may be one, even as we are one;*
>
> *I in them, and thou in me, that they may be made
> perfect in one; and that the world may know that thou
> hast sent me, and hast loved them, as thou hast loved
> me.*
>
> JOHN 17: 21, 23.

ONE OF MY MOST cherished privileges has been a
deep fellowship with hosts of people in the British
Isles, as down the years I have visited many villages,
towns and cities, bearing witness to Christ's love.

In our country we have some fifty-two million people packed
in islands only as big as one American state, and often smaller.
As in other civilised lands, the population is densely concentrated in towns and cities. And most of them—like London,
Edinburgh, Newcastle, Carlisle, Lancaster, York, Caernarvon,
Doncaster, Colchester, Winchester and many more—have
their roots in living history.

At Stonehenge, in Wiltshire, we can still behold the great
circle of stones which in the dim past was a Druid temple of
the ancient Britons. And at Glastonbury there is the ruined
Abbey standing on the site of the first Christian Church, a
crude wattle church, reported to have been founded by Joseph
of Arimathaea. I once spent several days in retreat and meditation in the crypt where the first altar stood, and captured

there much of the love of Christ which motivated those early bold disciples.

At Plymouth, not long ago, I stood on the Hoe and remembered the Pilgrim Fathers courageously setting out across the Atlantic in the *Mayflower*. Little did they then dream that they were the beginning of a movement of people destined to awaken as a mighty nation such as the United States of America is today!

Up and down our land we move through great industrial cities like Glasgow, Birmingham, Manchester, Coventry, Liverpool, Leeds and scores of other centres of culture and creativeness. And, in most of them, one can so quickly step from a modern block of offices to enter some medieval church, or walk along an ancient Roman roadway.

Right across the north of England, on the borders of Scotland, the Roman Wall is still a relic of considerable proportions. It wends its way over the wild hills and dales all the way from Carlisle in the west to Newcastle in the east, nearly a hundred miles of it. And once the Roman Empire built it to defend their colony of England from the marauding Scottish tribes to the north.

The Roman garrison towns of Hexham, Wallsend and Carlisle still show the signs of their growth through nearly two thousand years, as an ancient redwood tree in America testifies through its gnarled roots and towering trunk to the passing of the centuries.

Some time ago we visited the ruins of the Roman garrison town of Corstopitum, on the Wall, which had been excavated. It was astonishing to see the collection of arms, armour, shoes, shields, kitchen implements and all the paraphernalia of busy soldiering. And one could not help but realise, through these ornaments and utilities, how we all grew out of these men and women whose destiny it was to live in those days, and even in times long preceding them.

The museums and cities of the old world, whether they be in England or Egypt, India or Iraq, China or the Holy Land, serve as a constant reminder of the common identity of all people and the fact that, no matter how advanced we may be today, we are but the present product of a growth taking place through our long-lost forbears.

We are what we are today as much through the early struggles of a tribe in a jungle thousands of years ago, as through our own enterprise in the country where we happened to be born. And it is good to remember, if we live in a more advanced point of civilisation, that we could just as easily have been born in an African tribe or a Chinese village, forced by circumstance to take up life as it is expressed there.

It is singularly true that "There, but for the Grace of God, go I" as we behold any person, anywhere. Indeed, so clear is the revelation today that we are all one in each other through the Spirit of God, that we could truly say with spiritual vision "There, *by* the Grace of God, go I" for everyone, without exception in the inward reality, is a part of our own being.

In spite of the astonishing industrial and economic activity in the British Isles, and the vast towns and cities erected by the hundred to house it all, it is a beautiful land. Poets have written about "this England" in thousands of verses, seeking to describe our hills and dales, the green pastures and cool waters. They respond to the luxuriant growth and birdsong of springtime, and capture the ancient lore of a people who have sprung from the castles, farms, villages and cottages which so lavishly sprinkle the countryside outside the cities.

It is humbling to realise the inherent power of the Christian tradition in these Isles. Dedicated communities like Iona of the Scottish Western Isles, Lindisfarne on the Northumberland coast, Lee Abbey in the south-west and various others, still testify to their roots in ancient Christianity. And of course there are thousands of churches, many of them hundreds of years old, throughout the land.

Whether one visits Westminster Abbey in London, York Minster, Durham Cathedral, a score of other cathedrals, or the many ruined abbeys, one cannot escape witnessing the love, vision and power of a people who long ago raised this beautiful architecture, these prayers in stone, to the Glory of God.

It is a great inspiration to conduct a service in a centuries-old church. I recall, for example, sharing this joy on several occasions with my old friend, the Rev. Cecil Gibbings, in his ancient Anglican Church at Longthorpe, near Peterborough.

Passing through the portals, one stands in awe and reverence as the peace of generations of prayer opens the inward doors of the soul. The spirit leaps as it realises that worship has gone on in this Holy Place for nine hundred years, and captures something of the lives of mothers, fathers and their children coming and going within these walls for so many generations.

In our present time we are realising scientifically that everything is the product of invisible inward power, expressed more accurately in terms of energy and vibration, than matter as our senses apprehend it. We can, therefore, more easily understand the power of mind and the fact that thoughts are living things.

In such a place as Longthorpe Church, we do not even need the aid of science to point to the reality of the pervading "atmosphere". The Peace and Power are tangible to the senses and evoke an inward awareness of the imprinted love and prayer of countless people in the past. And one knows and feels, without instruction, the Presence of God.

Ancient pillars and pews, the relics of tattered flags of long forgotten armies, crests, ornaments and historical testaments, seem but to enhance the stability and enduring nature of the Christian Church everywhere. It is surely not astonishing, but natural, that the services we held at Longthorpe were replete with love, healings and changed lives.

The villages of this England are beautiful and their cottages and farmhouses, mellowed by many years, blend with the woods and hills, or nestle beside the cool rivers, in peace. Invariably, the rugged tower of the parish church can be seen amidst the trees, testifying to the Christ of every hamlet in the land. And nearby will be the Methodist, Baptist, Congregational or—especially in Scotland—the Presbyterian Church.

Sometimes I visit churches over the border, when these Scotsmen feel led to invite a mere "Sassenach", or Englishman, into their country! What wonderful times we have had with the Lord amongst their ministers and people!

When a Scotsman makes up his mind about anything, he will go forward with a rugged determination and perseverance which lead him to victory. This kind of vision and inward courage have sent them on enterprising work throughout the world. In fact, wherever one travels, east or west—even in the hinterland of plain, mountain or desert, from Peru to China —there will surely be a man from Scotland organising something!

In Glasgow I had rich fellowship with a fraternity of ministers who were intent on study and practising the cause of Divine Healing through Christ's Ministry. Like many other ministers throughout the world, they were responding to the vision and challenge of modern times to bring back the full Gospel into realistic operation.

As I conducted services in the Rev. Andrew Gordon's church, I remembered some weeks before watching and listening to him on a television programme, after the dedication ceremony opening his new church. He walked through the aisles and exposed the soul of all true Christians as he talked of the ideal, the meaning and reality of Christ's teaching as applied to life and its problems today. He was, at that moment, representing every one of the hundreds of thousands of Christian ministers throughout the world.

The Rev. Clarence Finlayson was in charge of the Church of Scotland at Pollok on the outskirts of Glasgow (he has now gone to Edinburgh). This dynamic, kind and learned man had created, through the Lord, a tremendous ministry. His church is always seething with activity, both in worship and in all the manifold undergirding work from youth club to men's fraternals and women's groups. And the Lord has surely been with us in our Divine healing services in that old church.

This Pollok area is a new suburb of Glasgow. Today the skyline is etched by skyscraper blocks of apartments built to house a host of people from the centre of the city, as the old property there became ready for clearance under improvement projects. As the people moved away from the centre, the church no longer had a congregation.

Rather than build a new church, these invincible Scotsmen took the huge old building down, stone by stone, and rebuilt it on the new site at Pollok! There it stands today, exact in every detail, to carry on its tradition of service, looking very dignified indeed among the modern mass of bricks and mortar. Americans have been known to move a castle or mansion stone by stone from England to the United States. I hope they never start on our churches!

No person in the British Isles, whether church member or not, could even begin to imagine life without all these churches as the background to the community of village, town or city. Despite all the frailties inherent in man or nation, and all the mistakes we make, it is still vital and significant that our roots are grounded, as a civilisation, in the Christian tradition. And this has always been the scaffolding within which, however inadequately, the entire structure of our national consciousness and achievement has arisen.

It is impossible here to indicate by name the host of ministers in this country, the United States, the British Commonwealth, in Europe and the world generally, who are leading the way into the New Age. It is enough to know they are there, and that God is forever drawing us all together into a common partnership with the stimulating vision of the high destiny of mankind.

The beloved "Mac", here in our Sanctuary, captured something of this in the inspired poem she presented to me the other day.

*   *   *   *

The Dawning Day

"And they shall be mine, saith the Lord of hosts, in that day when I make up my jewels" (Mal. 3: 17).

Above the clouds of hate and strife, on distant wastes afar
Shedding a ray of light and life, there gleamed a guiding Star.
O'er many a land, down direful years, its radiant message shone.
'Midst fogs of doubt and mists of tears, the glory lingered on;
And men have lived and men have died to tend the sacred flame.
Earth's darkened roads were glorified where'er the rapture came.

Now breaks the long-appointed day, with vision to the blind,
The Lord returns to show His Way to warring humankind.
Forth from the world He garners them. There is no creed nor sect,
For none shall conquer, none condemn, since all are His elect.
Brown hands clasps white in close caress, together they have trod
The paths that through the wilderness lead to the heights of God.

Behold the Living Church to be, no temple built with hands!
Upon the steeps of Calvary its stainless structure stands.
Here every nation bends the knee. God flings its portals wide,
And Jew and Gentile, bond and free, have each their place inside.
Its Law is Love, its sole commands the gain of selfless loss.
Upon its glimmering altar stands the symbol of the Cross.

The day is dawning, heralded by sunrise in the East,
When you shall share your brethren's cup, and Christ shall be your Priest.

I have sought, in prayer, to fill these pages with a witness. If I testify strongly, or with any sense of authority, please forgive me; for my sole intention, before God, has been to reveal what the Lord can do with our weak and wandering lives as we journey together in love with one another and with Him.

Of all people, I have such cause to know thankfully this miracle-working power. Since I left school in my early teens, I had little education in the academic sense. Subsequently, as a business man, I could only learn about life and its problems the hard way. But, like the fishermen of old, the Lord was able to take this very inadequate material and send me forth to preach the good news along the highways of the world.

These journeys are "miracles", no less than Divine healing, for they reveal the power of Christ to change a life and make it more useful, in a greater service, however expressed. It is not the man who becomes a "fisher of men", but the Lord Who does the "fishing" through him.

And, of course, no matter how wonderful Divine healing is (and none can doubt its importance) we should always regard it as a stepping stone to the other bank of the river where we need to dwell.

Fundamentally, we do not come to God to be healed, but rather to be transformed, to be made new creatures in Christ. Neither need we wait until our lives are broken before we partake of this feast.

Instead, with clearing vision, we should be quickened in our faith and understanding of Divine Law through the witness of those who have been healed by prayer, and leap to the Divine Awakening which beckons us on to fulfil the plans of God which are true to our personality and objectives.

When I was last in South Africa on a mission I met a Mrs. Viljoen. She had been healed in a remarkable way the previous year. I have reserved her witness for this last chapter because the way her healing came about was entirely through her own surrender to God.

By this I mean that although she attended services, it was through her own act of love and faith that she was healed in the Presence, as she was sharing in the service. It seems to symbolise all that has been written in this book, and surely points to the true possibilities inherent in all worship, in all churches, at any time.

I took the opportunity of recording the story in her own words. Her voice, with a strong Afrikaans accent, was vibrant with power as my tape-recorder imprinted it. We will gladly send this recording to anyone who desires a copy. It is Serial No. S.A.2. This is what she says:

"About four years ago I fell from a step and injured my spine, and the doctors took half a disc, which is worse than the whole disc, out of my spine, so naturally I had to be held up by a brace made here in the orthopaedic hospital. And for four years I was quite a miserable person, really miserable, because from one day to the next I never knew whether I could cope with it. I could never make plans because I never knew whether I could carry them out. Even in those years, Mrs. Gordon-Davis of the Grace Dieu Healing Sanctuary tried hard to convince me that I didn't have to suffer like that, that God could heal me. I tried, in my own simple way, but just carried on thinking, 'Well, I don't suppose I've got enough faith.'

"Then you came here and I'll never forget the morning when I first saw you. I had one thought in my mind. I was suffering, I was really miserable. But I had an old friend of many years. She was just a skeleton with a skin over her. And I always thought, 'Well, she suffers more than I do.' And when I was told about the meeting that was going to be held on the Thursday morning, the thought struck me, 'I must try to get her to the service.'

"That was my first thought, and then with my spine being so painful I didn't know how I was going to get there, because she was practically an invalid. So I thought, 'Well, God will get her there somehow. He will make some sort of a plan.' And sure enough we got her there to the service. I was so pleased because she was sitting in the front row and thought, 'Oh, that's lovely. You *must* see her.' And when I was asked: 'Aren't you going to be in the Sanctuary too?' I answered: 'No. I don't want to take up space for anybody who needs it more than I do.' I thought I'd just stay at the back on the porch so that I could perhaps hear what you said and also see you.

"So I was there at the back, and you started. It's difficult to explain what happened to me, because as you spoke I felt smaller and smaller and smaller. I was practically crawling in the dust. So I thought to myself, 'Well, I always knew I wasn't a good person, but I never knew I was that bad.' I felt terrible. And then you attended to the people inside, and eventually came to the back. You said, 'Is there anyone for healing here?' I looked at you and thought, 'I could bluff myself very easily, and I could bluff you. But one thing I know—*I could never bluff God.*' I was not ready for healing. I knew it then, because I knew that you as a person could not heal me. Only God could heal and I had to get all the channels open for Him.

"So I walked home. Oh, what a walk—I felt terrible! When I came home my daughter, Girlie, was all excited and said, 'Oh, were you there? Did you see Brother Mandus?' And I said, 'Yes, but I don't want to talk about it.' She was very disappointed. She didn't know why. Oh, but I was crawling in the dust. I thought, 'Well, if I don't get healed then I deserve not to be because I've been such a terrible, horrible person; bearing malice, hating people and disliking them. It's just not good enough.'

"On the Saturday night when you held your first meeting in the Trinity Methodist Church, I was there. I was so keen to go, but was still crawling in the dust. I didn't want to sit too near the front. I didn't want people to see how I suffered. I sat right in the middle. You talked about love and forgiveness. But, you see, there was one person that I didn't like—and as you also explained on the Thursday morning, we must love everybody. And I said, 'Well, that's all right. I can love everybody, but I still don't like that person.' So that night at Trinity you explained to us that if there should be a person that we couldn't love, or if that person has done something wrong to hurt us or to make us disgusted with life—it is not in our power to judge, it should be left to God to judge that person. And for me, I should offer only love.

"You said that night that if we could do that, and get direct contact with God, we could be healed. And I thought to myself, 'Isn't that just my life? Well, then, I'll leave her entirely to God.' And I sat in the church and I said, 'Right. Here I am, and You know how bad I am. I'm a miserable sort of person, but can You do anything for me? My spine is practically broken. If You'll mend me, my spine, I'm here for Your use. If I'm any good to You, here I am.'

"Then I felt a hot glow as if something had touched my hip, and it went through my body. With the spine practically broken, the tips of my lungs through so much lying down were drying up, and I always had great pain in my chest. As I sat in the church you never knew anything about me. As you were talking, telling us how to be healed, I just applied your teaching.

"I said to God, 'Well, here I am.' As you were talking, it suddenly happened. I was sitting there in pain because as I sit the steel of the brace presses on the seat. I was uncomfortable—I was always uncomfortable. After that experience I instantly knew that I was healed. Immediately this brace felt very heavy on me, and I wanted to take it off there and then.

"My daughter, Girlie, was sitting next to me and I said to her, 'Girlie, I'm healed.' She never doubted—she never doubted for a second. And she said, 'Oh, Mam, that's beautiful.' I said, 'Yes, it is.' And you know, I got up. Usually we have to catch a bus home. I said to Girlie, 'Oh, I wish I could get this brace off.' She said, 'Shall we catch the bus?' I said, 'No. For the first time in four years I can walk with my legs free. Look at this.' And I walked down the street—I was so free. It was too lovely!

"I've always said since that night that the strongest part of my body is my spine. Previously, the doctor gave me no hope whatsoever to live a normal life. I couldn't keep house, I couldn't do anything, and they emphasised how very, very careful I would have to be, because the first time I had a fall I would be paralysed. They said, 'Well, Mrs. Viljoen, you are one of the people that we doctors cannot heal. You will have to accept the fact that you will be as you are and the spine will definitely deteriorate.'

"Then, after the healing, I went to the same doctor who had operated, and said, 'Do you remember me?' And he looked at me and said, 'Yes I do. I operated on your spine,' and asked, 'How are you?' And I said, 'Well, I've been pretty miserable for four years, but now I am perfect.' He confirmed that. I bent double in front of him to demonstrate it."

*   *   *   *

I was very grateful for this woman's witness because the significance of her experience potentially touches the well-being of every person on earth.

Spiritually, or scientifically, we must face the facts as presented. As in the miracles of Jesus and the disciples, God was able to move in the midst of a mind, open a way, and then motivate bones, nerves and tissues in a woman's spine to re-set them in the pattern of Divine order which He implanted, even while Mrs. Viljoen was a seed in her mother's womb.

If it can happen once, it can occur a million times. The moment man was able to harness electricity, and make one electric lamp, it became a realistic project to light the homes of every city on earth. Yet, if a broken wire stops the flow of current, all the electricity in the world would not light even one lamp in that circuit.

Since we live in a world governed by Divine Laws, it is

obvious that we can only live successfully when we seek to understand them and conform to their purpose. No seaman would venture across the oceans without a chart and compass. And it is highly dangerous for man, or nation, to embark on his travels through Eternity without knowing the magnitude of the adventure and without a Light to show the way.

The next phase of evolution is now awakening because countless people realise that we can no longer dare to ignore either the dangers or the means whereby we can achieve our true objectives. But the awakening multitudes represent the dedication and purpose of the individual, one by one, as he or she sees the Light.

Therefore, in every forward movement of the race, we should concentrate on the essential nature of personal awakening. We are not to be content to leave it to other intangible and unknown churches and groups, or other people, but rather to become that Light in Christ ourselves. Then we can be inspired, guided and stimulated by the work of others, and go forward with greater enterprise and enthusiasm to fulfil our personal part of the Plan.

In this way the Lord will lead us, ministry and laity alike, to be about the Father's Business, and the repercussions will sweep through the entire society.

The vision for the New Age is nothing less than a realistic partnership with Christ in the very centre of every human activity. The day will dawn, inevitably, when the people throughout the world will give allegiance to the Father first in all things, and the Kingdom of God will be established in the hearts and minds of men on earth, as it already is in heaven. That is what Jesus proclaimed. Today we know He was right, spiritually and scientifically, and can therefore proceed with confidence to awaken to the truth that will make all men free.

Whether it takes a hundred, a thousand or ten thousand years to bring into full realisation will only depend on how quickly, one by one, we can become receptive to the Divine Idea. At this time, we see only the second dawn of the new era. Jesus brought the Light; now the clouds are clearing on the horizon. Soon that Light will be seen by more and more people and, even as an intellectual evolution has quickened, so shall we begin to leap forward spiritually to release the urgently needed balance.

Some day, in the distant future, the happy, healthy, illumined and prosperous people of that time will look back down the years to assess our present degree of civilisation. The historians, philosophers and spiritual teachers will sadly realise the barbarism and immaturity of our vaunted civilisation.

They will point to our arts and crafts, and all the signs of a growing culture, and wonder at so many of our achievements. The scientist will marvel with great interest as he reads of man's first rockets orbiting the earth, and the subsequent space-ships which eventually began to explore the planetary system.

But in that greater day of the noonday sun of spiritual knowledge and peace the children at school will also be shown how their present civilisation rose out of the hopes and dreams of man, as well as from his failures. Through the perspective of time, they will see how, beginning with Jesus, people gradually commenced to awaken to the living truth.

Their teachers, with sure knowledge, will point to the spiritual leaders who arose out of the darkness and through teaching, prayer, Divine healing and true vision, began to open the way along which all humanity subsequently streamed.

The people of the future will inherit what we initiate, and it becomes increasingly imperative that we, of this very special generation, should proceed boldly to pioneer the way through the jungles of sin and ignorance which confine the whole race of mankind.

Now is the time for individual as well as collective spiritual enterprise. We must teach our young people now that the greatest of all adventures lies in an exploration of Divine Power. We must take our appointed part in being channels of information about these great objectives, by sharing our books and recordings with others who are seeking the Light.

This is no time for apathy and complacency. People need information, instruction and experience. Every man, every woman, who receives knowledge of spiritual truth has, before God, the immediate responsibility of passing it on to someone else. Great works always stem from the work of the individual, and you who read these words, if they spell truth to you, will also save someone else's life through you!

Christ asks us to go all the way with Him. In this, we are told not to count the cost in sacrifice or service, but to become so filled with His Spirit that His good works radiate through us as a light to everyone else.

To be born today, at this critical and dangerous time in history, is a privilege indeed. Far better to be in the midst of vital issues and adventures, than to be a sheep in a field doing nothing but eat the grass. It is far more rewarding to live dangerously in a great cause than to shut out the dynamics of life itself, bolstered only by the little ego and its cherished possessions.

This is a time for men and women of good will and vision personally to reveal the Christ Way in their homes, offices, factories, arts and churches.

We only fail for lack of knowledge about the greater truth.

Therefore, without being a preacher or leader, you can immediately be the Lord's instrument to bring release to others. There is a mass of powerful writing available on this entire subject by hundreds of people who are reporting their own experience and seeking to share it with all.

Look for these good works, and do not be afraid to spend money on truth that is priceless. But do not search for yourself alone. Be on fire with a new sense of mission, and obtain the books indicated by your guidance to give them away in LOVE, unconditionally, to those who may be likewise awakened through your gift to God, even as you may have found your freedom through His gift to you.

In these days, the way is made so easy for those who would serve. They no longer need to be trained preachers to lead people home to Him. The witnessing work is already in print and on tape, waiting only for millions of people to bear it into the world with reverent hands to rescue the sick and weary ones still wandering in the wilderness.

If, for example, by some miracle, every person on earth became filled with enthusiasm and dedication to do just this one act of service, and inspire others to do the same, the spiritual scene in the entire world would be revolutionised within a decade, never mind a century or a thousand years.

We need today not just a few illumined people, but millions of them, all taking an honest and dedicated part in the general awakening. Like the Christians of the Coliseum and catacombs of Rome, we are challenged and invited to give our all in fellowship with one another in Christ's service.

For too long our approach to spiritual teaching has been to see if this or that method might prosper our own personal lives. The vision of Christ, as always, for the New Age now dawning is the laying down of our self-interest as we fervently give our thoughts, prayers, activity and money to look for lost souls.

In our hospitals alone lie a lost army of our brothers and sisters, to say nothing of all those who lie sick or crippled at home.

In the light of our present vision, it is no idle statement to say that if every patient in a hospital knew the truth you are reading, there would be a tremendous increase in healing on every level. Our hospitals should be living Power Stations of Prayer, based on the highest concepts of love and faith. Doctors, nurses, patients, ministers and congregations should even now, with the spiritual knowledge available, be embarked on the most potent healing mission in history.

It is lack of knowledge, lack of belief, which hold us back. And the only way to get this knowledge to parents, teachers, children, doctors, patients, business men and politicians, is to get it into ever greater circulation by means of the written or spoken word of witness.

Spiritual work today can no longer be circumscribed by the walls of a church. We are all invited to embark on a world ministry, centred in the church, but reaching out into the environment where people are living. And this, as always, requires the help of people who will make their own lives the Father's Business.

"Therefore said he unto them, The harvest truly is great, but the labourers are few: pray ye therefore the Lord of the harvest, that he would send forth labourers into his harvest" (Luke 10: 2).

I do not believe you would even be reading these words unless you were either already serving or were ready to do so. And it is always a simple truth to say that, whoever we are, you or I or anyone, whatever we are doing today is but a door opening to something bigger and better that we can do tomorrow, especially if we unite together in the Father to do it.

The secret of Love in all its potency lies in giving, not getting. The things we need are then spontaneously added unto us. The world is dying for the lack of people who are prepared to believe this, live it and teach it.

*   *   *   *

I am still sitting in my car on the promenade writing this book, and now coming to the end of it. Many tides have ebbed and flowed over the sands while I have been writing. Rainstorms and sunshine have bathed the winter scene. But the Lord has been with me as I sought only to be the channel of His Love to you.

In His Spirit, and through this book, I shall be meeting you, wherever you may be, and only the Father will have arranged the meeting place. You may live in California or South Africa, or in a cottage in an English village. You may be a queen on a throne or a fisherman on the sea. But rich or poor, sick or well, coloured or white, whoever or wherever you are, God knows you and loves you and, in the end, that is all any of us need to understand.

I hope we may meet personally some day. I pray, with all my heart and soul, that these words have helped you towards our common goal, and that they may also bring blessings to others through your service and mine; for I love you too.

Thank You, Father, in the Name of our Lord and Saviour Jesus Christ, to Whom be all Honour and Glory.

"That they all may be one; as thou, Father, art in me, and I in thee, that they also may be one in us; that the world may believe that thou hast sent me."

This is the Divine Awakening!

*　　　*　　　*　　　*

Thank you, Father, for the love and dedication down the years of all those disciples who have so lovingly served thee in our Sanctuary.

Thank you, Lord, for the friendship and faith of so many ministers and friends throughout the world who have crusaded with us in this vision for the new Christ Age.

In love and humility, Father, we all offer our lives to Thee. Take us, one by one, and reconsecrate us to the complete fulfilment of Thy Will, through Jesus Christ our Lord, that we may continue to serve Thee and take our part in bringing healing and love to all whose lives touch ours.

Thank you, Father, for Perfect Everything for all mankind, and for our own lives, now, and unto all eternity. Amen.

The Christ Within

He touches the dumb, and torrents of pent-up love pour from their lips;

He breathes on the lame, and they dance to the music of life;

He understands all you can ever utter, and knows the answers to all your questions.

He has all you need and everything you will ever need at any time, anywhere, in this world or in any of the myriad mansions of the Universal Mind.

If you failed before, He will show you how to succeed.

If your last hope expired in the grave of love, He will revive the hope and rekindle the love.

If you fell from the height to which you had climbed, He will tenderly raise you aloft and restore your inheritance.

And though all others forsake you, He will never forsake you.

He is the reality you have glimpsed in your most inspired moments,

The full tide of the rapture you have experienced in waves,

And the whole heaven of the love you have dimly imagined in your loftiest dreams.

He is the invisible companion of your days and nights, your Protector and Guardian Angel,

The bridegroom of your soul and the bride of your spirit.

At His word the Everlasting Gates lift up their heads and the Everlasting Doors swing open,

To reveal the heaven of your dreams,

Your immortal heritage and peculiar treasure, distilled from the ages,

The nectar crushed from the blooms of countless lives in countless worlds,

Your marriage portion,

When you are aware of His presence, heaven is empty,

And when He folds you in His arms, you yourself are heaven, for He is with you.

When you listen to His voice the whole world is silent, and when you look into His eyes, the sun and moon are no more.

His power is more stable than the earth under your feet, and you rest in His glory as a child in its mother's womb.

His life is the chariot of fire in which your spirit travels whithersoever it will,

And His love is the seamless robe you will wear after your espousal;

And His light is the divine ether in which you live, move, and have your being in heaven and upon earth, throughout the ages.

MEREDITH STARR

45
49
166